RED WINGS
ESSENTIAL

Everything You Need to Know
to Be a Real Fan!

Nicholas J. Cotsonika

TRIUMPH
BOOKS

Library of Congress Cataloging-in-Publication Data

Cotsonika, Nicholas J.
    Red Wings essential : everything you need to know to be a real fan! / Nicholas J. Cotsonika.
        p. cm.
    ISBN-13: 978-1-57243-757-9
    ISBN-10: 1-57243-757-X
        1. Detroit Red Wings (Hockey team)—Anecdotes. 2. Detroit Red Wings (Hockey team)—Miscellanea. I. Title.

GV848.D47C68 2005
796.962'64'0977434—dc22

                                                        2005050611

        3 9082 10252 1013

This book is available in quantity at special discounts for your group or organization. For further information, contact:

Triumph Books
542 South Dearborn Street
Suite 750
Chicago, Illinois 60605
(312) 939-3330
Fax (312) 663-3557

Printed in U.S.A.
ISBN-13: 978-1-57243-757-9
ISBN-10: 1-57243-757-X
Design by Patricia Frey
All photos courtesy of AP/Wide World Photos except where otherwise indicated

Contents

Humble Beginnings

Once upon a time, the Red Wings weren't the Red Wings.

Detroit's hockey history began with Charles Hughes, a sportswriter and schmoozer who once served as Teddy Roosevelt's public relations man. He helped persuade the city's power brokers to build the Detroit Athletic Club in 1915 and to hire him as its manager. Then, in 1926, he convinced his contacts at the club that the city needed a professional hockey franchise if it wanted serious consideration as a big-league town.

Hughes rounded up 73 local investors, including industrialist Edsel Ford, department store magnate S. S. Kresge, and newspaper publisher William Scripps. The group paid the NHL a $100,000 franchise fee, then paid another $100,000 to purchase the rights to 15 members of the Victoria Cougars, a Western Hockey League club that had won the 1925 Stanley Cup. Hughes signed nine of the players to contracts, including player/manager Art Duncan and superstar forward Frank Fredrickson. He kept Cougars as the team name, thinking that it was an appropriate continuation of the theme set by the Tigers.

The Cougars' first season was anything but spectacular. They were a permanent road team in 1926–1927, playing home games at the six-thousand-seat Border Cities Arena across the Detroit River in Windsor, Ontario, while waiting for the million-dollar Olympia Stadium to be built at Grand River and McGraw. They lost their November 18 debut to the Boston Bruins, 2–0, shuffled their aging lineup extensively, and finished 12–28–4.

Dead last.

Smarting from an $84,000 loss, Hughes, in desperation, asked NHL president Frank Calder for help in finding a coach and general manager. Word traveled throughout the league, and it reached the ears of Jack

Adams, a sometimes gruff, sometimes gregarious 32-year-old who had served as a forward and assistant coach with the Cup-winning Ottawa Senators.

Adams brashly called Calder and said, "I'm the man for the Detroit job!" Calder, taken aback, took him at his word and arranged for an interview with Hughes, in which Adams told Hughes what he had told Calder so bluntly before.

"I'd been involved in winning the Stanley Cup for Ottawa," Adams said in Stan Fischler's *Motor City Muscle*, "so I told Hughes that he needed me more than I needed him."

TRIVIA

In 1930 the three Detroit daily newspapers—the *Free Press, News*, and *Times*—held a contest to pick a new name for the franchise. The Cougars were renamed the Falcons. Which of these nicknames wasn't among the finalists?

A. Trojans
B. Wanderers
C. Magnetos
D. Dynamos

Answers to the trivia questions are on pages 185–186.

Hughes couldn't argue with Adams, a hockey vagabond who once played with a professional team in Calumet, Michigan, with Notre Dame football legend George Gipp. So Hughes hired him, and Adams went to work immediately. Among Adams's first moves was injecting young legs into his lineup. He acquired a small, combative winger named Larry Aurie, whom he soon was fond of calling "the best two-way player in hockey."

The Cougars opened the 1927–1928 season on the road with a 6–0 victory in Pittsburgh and a 5–2 loss in Boston, then competed on Detroit ice for the first time. The opening game at Olympia was a festive affair. A standing-room-only crowd of more than ten thousand was there. So was mayor John Smith, who presented Adams with bunches of chrysanthemums. So was the Michigan band, which played throughout the game. So was a group of figure skaters, who performed between periods. So was Foster Hewitt—the first man to make the call "He shoots! He scores!"—who broadcast the game on the radio station WGHP.

The Cougars lost to Ottawa, 2–1, but weren't discouraged. Improving under Adams, they finished the season 19–19–6 and barely missed the playoffs. Next season, they finished 19–16–9, made the playoffs for the first time, and pulled in a tidy $175,000 profit. Aurie and center Ebenezer

Jack Adams (front row, fourth from left) led Detroit's NHL franchise through the Depression to the elation of its first Stanley Cup in 1936.

"Ebbie" Goodfellow held great promise for the future. Things were going quite well.

But then the Depression hit. Attendance plummeted so badly that Adams went door-to-door on Grand River trying to sell tickets and even allowed a fan into a charity exhibition one night for five bags of potatoes.

"We took his spuds," Adams said in Fischler's book, "and gave him standing room."

The Cougars' performance in 1929–1930 matched the economic malaise: they went 14–24–6 and missed the playoffs again.

After the season, the team tried to drum up interest by holding a contest in the newspapers to determine a new name. The fans chose Falcons. New uniforms with gold letters were introduced, marking the only time the team would wear a color other than red and white.

By the NUMBERS $100,000—Franchise fee the original group of investors—which included Edsel Ford, S. S. Kresge, and William E. Scripps—paid to establish an NHL team in Detroit in 1926. It is also the amount James Norris paid for the financially troubled franchise, its farm team, and Olympia Stadium in 1932.

TRIVIA

Where did the Red Wings first play their home games?

A. Border Cities Arena
B. Navin Field
C. Olympia Stadium
D. Joe Louis Arena

Answers to the trivia questions are on pages 185–186.

But the hoopla failed to make an impact. The Falcons finished in last place in 1930–1931, then lost to the Montreal Maroons in the first round in 1931–1932—then almost ceased to exist because of financial problems.

By the spring of 1932, the team had defaulted on its mortgage, and its property had been put into receivership—even though Adams had been so tight with money that players weren't allowed to travel in sleeping cars on road trips and ate cheese sandwiches wrapped in wax paper for meals. Investors kept their hands in their pockets. The Olympia was padlocked.

"We were this depressed: if Howie Morenz, the great Montreal star, had been available for $1.98, we couldn't have afforded him," Adams said in Fischler's book.

The team needed help. It needed James Norris. A Montreal native and ardent puckhead, Norris had moved to Chicago and become a millionaire in the grain business. But the 53-year-old tycoon missed hockey badly and yearned for an NHL franchise, whether in the Windy City, where he already owned an interest in Chicago Stadium, or anywhere else. When the opportunity arose to buy the Detroit team for $100,000, Norris pounced on it—and put pressure on Adams.

"I'll give you a year on probation," Norris told Adams, "with no contract."

Norris was known as "Pops" to distinguish him from his oldest son, James Jr., who became a co-owner of the Chicago Black Hawks in 1946. And like any Pops, he was no-nonsense. He got his way. An innovative man, Norris solidified the team's identity with one bold move.

Borrowing the name and emblem of a team for which he used to play, the Montreal Winged Wheelers, he renamed the Falcons the Red Wings, figuring the blood-red sweaters and unique crest would fit in well with the Motor City's image.

"Pops was the bankroll and the boss," Adams said in Richard Bak's *Detroit Red Wings: The Illustrated History.* "After he took over, Detroit hockey never looked back."

The Link

He sat in the Olympia Room at Joe Louis Arena, cradling a cup of coffee in his hands, surrounded by black-and-white pictures of Red Wings past. Harry Lumley. Carl Liscombe. Marcel Pronovost. Marty Pavelich. And on and on.

"I knew them all," he said.

So he did.

Wally Crossman was known as "the Link," because in spending an astonishing 61 seasons as a dressing-room assistant, he connected the team to its history unlike any of its other employees.

Crossman came from Ontario to Michigan with his family in 1926, the year Detroit entered the NHL. He lived near old Olympia Stadium—*new* Olympia Stadium, that is. When Crossman arrived, there was just a hole in the ground at Grand River and McGraw. He watched workers build the basement, install the brine pipes, and lay red brick after red brick.

After the Olympia opened in 1927, Crossman was a fixture. He worked as a soda jerk at a neighborhood drug store, so he was never far away. He sat in the balcony for 25 cents. He went to practice for free.

"I just hung around and hung around," Crossman said. "I'd go into the building and get acquainted with all the players and the coaches."

In 1940 war duty called the Wings' dressing-room assistant, and coach/general manager Jack Adams asked Crossman if he would fill in.

"I've been carrying on for him ever since," Crossman said.

Crossman also married in 1940. So perhaps it's poetic that the only jewelry he ever wore was a Wings championship ring from the fifties on his left ring finger. The ring had a slender gold band, with a red stone and a Winged Wheel, decorated by a single small diamond.

Four—Times a Red Wing has won the Selke Trophy as the NHL's best defensive forward:

Name	Season
Sergei Fedorov	1993–1994
Sergei Fedorov	1995–1996
Steve Yzerman	1999–2000
Kris Draper	2003–2004

Never receiving a paycheck—just a pair of tickets to every game and a tip from players at season's end—Crossman cared only about being part of the team and its tradition. And he *was* part of the team.

Mike Braham, the security guard outside the dressing room, said that the players each gave Crossman a fist-bump when they headed to the ice and that Crossman, who worked one of the bench doors, often gave them pats on the back.

In appreciation, the players sang "Happy Birthday" to Crossman in the dressing room when he turned 90 on October 30, 2000.

"I've been saying I would quit for the last four or five years, and every time training camp comes around, I'm at training camp," Crossman said.

"I could be in a rocking chair, wasting my time away, but I feel pretty good. Fortunately, my genes are working for me."

Crossman finally said good-bye in October 2002 so he could spend more time with his ailing wife, Peg.

"I've smelled enough sweat," he said, smiling. "I don't want to stay here till I'm 100. That's too long."

TRIVIA

When did the Red Wings play their first New Year's Eve game?

A. 1926
B. 1927
C. 1936
D. 1949

Answers to the trivia questions are on pages 185–186.

Sergei Fedorov (left), battling Winnipeg's Keith Tkachuk, was just one of the Red Wings stars Wally Crossman served in his 61 seasons as a dressing-room assistant.

A Huge Save

Goaltender Alex Connell made perhaps the biggest save in franchise history in the 1931–1932 season. He saved his own skin.

Connell spent 12 seasons in the NHL, and the Hall of Famer was best known for the shutout streak he had in 1927–1928 with the Ottawa Senators—a record six straight games, not allowing a puck past him for 446 minutes and 9 seconds. His career goals-against average of 1.91 ties with George Hainsworth for the lowest in league history.

He spent only one season with Detroit—the team was then called the Falcons—but his stay was memorable because of what happened one March night in New York. Richard Bak detailed the incident in his book *Detroit Red Wings: The Illustrated History.*

The Falcons faced the New York Americans in a game that would determine whether the New Yorkers would make the playoffs. It was tied at 1 in overtime when the Americans' Red Dutton fired a shot that appeared to go past Connell and in and out of the Detroit net.

The goal judge lit the red lamp, and the Americans started celebrating. But the referee disallowed the goal, certain the puck never went in. In the ensuing commotion, the goal judge had a few choice words for Connell—and Connell responded by punching him right in the nose.

Bad move.

The Americans were owned by a notorious bootlegger named Bill Dwyer, and the goal judge just so happened to be known as one of Dwyer's triggermen.

"Evidently his fingers on the red-light switch were as fast as his fingers on the trigger," Connell said later.

The game ended in a tie. Connell noticed a bunch of policemen pushing back the crowd as he went to the dressing room. Then two detectives paid him a visit. He was given an escort back to the hotel and was told to stay in his room until the team left town the next day.

But despite knowing his life was in danger, Connell went out for a sandwich with a friend, because the friend happened to be in town.

Again, bad move.

TRIVIA

Who was the first Red Wing to score 50 goals in a season?

A. Gordie Howe
B. Frank Mahovlich
C. Mickey Redmond
D. Marcel Dionne

Answers to the trivia questions are on pages 185–186.

Terry Sawchuk was famously moody, but he looks happy here after shutting out Montreal to win the 1955 Stanley Cup.

TOP TEN

Red Wings Goaltending Records
in Order of Wins

		Games	Record	GAA
1.	Terry Sawchuk	734	352–244–130	2.46
2.	Chris Osgood	421	241–116–46	2.43
3.	Harry Lumley	324	163–107–54	2.73
4.	Roger Crozier	310	130–119–43	2.94
5.	Tim Cheveldae	264	128–93–30	3.39
6.	Greg Stefan	299	115–127–30	3.92
7.	Manny Legace	180	112–34–16	2.39
8.	Jim Rutherford	314	97–165–43	3.68
9.	Roy Edwards	221	95–74–34	2.94
10.	Norm Smith	178	76–68–34	2.34

Connell was followed by some men who were up to no good, and as he sat in a diner near the hotel, he was asked, "Aren't you Alex Connell, goalkeeper for the Detroit Falcons?"

Goalies have to react quickly, and react quickly Connell did. He said not only was he not Alex Connell, he had never *heard* of the Detroit Falcons.

Great move. Smart move. Life-saving move.

The men let him go.

A few years later, a New York reporter told Connell that the gangsters who had approached him that night had met untimely ends. When Connell asked what had happened, the reporter replied, "Bang! Bang!"

The Longest Game

His name was Mud. But one night in 1936—make that one morning—he was a hockey hero.

In the first round of the playoffs against the Montreal Maroons, the defending Stanley Cup champions, the Red Wings survived a five-hour, 51-minute, six-overtime marathon and won, 1–0. Maroons goaltender Lorne Chabot made 61 saves, but Wings goaltender Normie Smith made 90.

The showdown ended at 2:25 AM, when forward Modere "Mud" Bruneteau, a seldom-used rookie recalled from the minors just two weeks earlier, drove to the net, accepted a pass from Hec Kilrea, and scored the game winner.

In the end, after what turned out to be the longest game of the century, even the puck was too exhausted to move.

"It was the funniest thing," Bruneteau said. "The puck just stuck there in the twine and didn't fall on the ice."

Bruneteau grinned at the Montreal Forum crowd while jamming money into his gloves and sweater, given to him by appreciative fans happy just to have the game over. He told reporters that he hoped his father, who never appreciated anything he did, had been listening on the radio at home in Manitoba.

The team went out to celebrate.

"I really found out how tired I was afterward when we went to the Lumberjacks Club in Montreal, and I had one bottle of ale," Smith said. "That set me right back on my heels."

But Bruneteau was wide-awake in his room at the Windsor Hotel at 5:00 AM.

Someone knocked on the door. Bruneteau got up and opened it.

Four—Times a Red Wing has won the Conn Smythe Trophy as the NHL playoffs' most valuable player:

Name	Year
Roger Crozier	1966
Mike Vernon	1997
Steve Yzerman	1998
Nicklas Lidstrom	2002

In the hallway stood Chabot.

"Sorry to bother you, kid," the goaltender said. "But you forgot something when you left the rink."

Chabot flipped Bruneteau the puck with which he had scored the game-winning goal, and with that, the Wings launched their first Ice Age. They finished a three-game sweep of the Maroons and beat the Toronto Maple Leafs in the finals, 3–1, winning their first Cup.

"There were no TV cameras then," forward Pete Kelly said in Richard Bak's *Detroit Red Wings: The Illustrated History.* "We didn't parade around the ice with the Cup. It was presented to us later, at the Royal York Hotel [in Toronto]. There were quite a few fans from Detroit crowded in there, I remember."

For the first time, Detroit had gone Cup crazy.

"When we got back to Detroit after the game, the town had gone wild," defenseman Ebbie Goodfellow said. "There seemed to be thousands of people at the railway station, and we were driven in a procession to Olympia, where another celebration took place."

The momentum of the victory carried into 1937. The Wings beat the Montreal Canadiens and the New York Rangers in five games apiece to become the first American team to win two consecutive Cups.

Jack Adams hadn't made so many moves after the Red Wings won the 1955 Stanley Cup, their fourth Cup in six years, Detroit's dynasty might have continued. Not wanting things to get stagnant, as they had after the back-to-back Cups of 1936 and 1937, Adams overhauled the roster. The Wings waited 42 years for their next championship.

Howe about That?

The Red Wings can thank the hockey gods for giving them Gordie Howe. Had things worked out differently in the beginning, Howe would have been a New York Ranger. Had they worked out differently on another occasion, Howe would have been dead.

In 1942, at the age of 14, Howe attended a New York Rangers tryout school in Winnipeg, Manitoba. He was homesick for Floral, Saskatchewan, a prairie town nine miles east of Saskatoon, where he lived a life of deprivation and poverty as one of nine children. He didn't play well at all. In a few brief whirls on the ice, he did nothing exceptional, and the Rangers blew a golden opportunity.

They sent him back to Saskatchewan.

Unsigned.

A year later, Wings scout Fred Pinckney invited Howe to a Detroit tryout camp in Windsor, Ontario, and even bought him his first suit for the trip. Already 6' and nearly 200 pounds at age 15, Howe displayed his extraordinary skills. He was ambidextrous, and that caught the eye of coach and general manager Jack Adams.

"Who's the big kid?" Adams said.

The Wings didn't make the same mistake the Rangers did.

Impressed, Adams arranged for Howe to work out with a junior team in Galt, Ontario. As part of the deal, Adams promised Howe a Wings jacket.

"I wanted that jacket so bad all the time I was in Galt," Howe said in Richard Bak's *Detroit Red Wings: The Illustrated History*. "I remember that quite a few times I walked down to the railroad station by myself. I knew when the Red Wings' train would be coming through town, traveling to games. I'd just wait there for them. I figured that if they stopped

Hockey has had many great players. But none has matched Gordie Howe's combination of scoring ability, toughness, intimidation, and longevity.

IF ONLY . . . a Sault Ste. Marie Greyhound hadn't already had No. 9 in 1977–1978, Red Wings great Gordie Howe wouldn't have been the genesis for hockey's two most recognizable numbers. Wayne Gretzky grew up idolizing Howe and wanted to wear his number in juniors, but because it was unavailable, he took No. 99. Mario Lemieux later copied it, flipped it, and turned it into No. 66.

for anything, I'd go aboard and see if I could ask Adams about my jacket. But the train never stopped. They went rolling through every time. I'd just walk back home."

In 1945 Howe was invited to training camp with the Wings, bunking in Olympia Stadium because of the wartime housing shortage. He amused himself by killing rats with his stick. After scoring two goals in an exhibition game in Akron, Ohio, he signed his first contract to play for the Wings' farm club in Omaha, Nebraska. He scored 22 goals there. In 1946 he made the big-league team for good—and approached Adams about some unfinished business.

"Mr. Adams," he said. "It has been two years now, and I haven't got my jacket yet."

Adams sent Howe, along with forwards Ted Lindsay and Marty Pavelich, to a sporting goods store downtown and told him to sign for it.

"It was smooth like satin on the outside, with leather sleeves and an alpaca lining," Howe said in Bak's book. "It had a big *D* with 'Red Wings' written on it. It looked like the most beautiful jacket in the world."

Had an incident in 1950 turned out for the worse, Howe wouldn't have been able to enjoy his prized jacket for very long.

In the playoff opener, the Wings trailed the Toronto Maple Leafs at Olympia Stadium in the second period, 3–0. Howe charged toward Leafs captain Ted "Teeder" Kennedy, but, as he lunged to hit him, Kennedy pulled up. Howe missed him and went hurtling headfirst into the boards, right in front of the Detroit bench.

As the crowd watched in stunned silence, paramedics placed Howe on a stretcher and rushed him to the

TRIVIA

What is a Gordie Howe hat trick?

A. Three goals
B. Three points
C. A goal, an assist, and a fight
D. A goal, an assist, and a beer

Answers to the trivia questions are on pages 185–186.

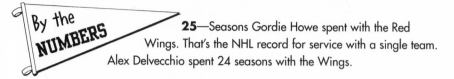

25—Seasons Gordie Howe spent with the Red Wings. That's the NHL record for service with a single team. Alex Delvecchio spent 24 seasons with the Wings.

hospital. He had broken his nose, shattered his cheekbone, seriously scratched his right eye, and possibly fractured his skull. His brain was hemorrhaging. He was in critical condition. His mother was flown in.

At 1:00 AM, neurosurgeon Fredric Shreiber saved Howe and a hockey town's hopes. He drilled an opening in Howe's skull and drained fluid to relieve pressure on his brain. Afterward, he put Howe in an oxygen tent.

By morning, Howe's condition had stabilized and improved. He pulled through, the only lingering effects of the operation being a facial tic, which earned him the nickname "Blinky." As the story goes, while he lay on the hospital gurney, he even apologized to coach Tommy Ivan for not playing better.

The Wings brawled brutally with the Leafs the next game, advanced to the Stanley Cup Finals, and beat the Rangers in seven games, when reserve left wing Pete Babando scored in double overtime.

The Olympia shook with excitement as the fans chanted, "We want Howe! We want Howe!" until Howe appeared in street clothes. Then the fans laughed as Lindsay pulled off Howe's hat—revealing the bald spot where Howe had been shaved for surgery—and threw it into the stands.

The Octopus

Al Sobotka sat on a table outside his office one night in April 2001. He had handled one of the first octopi of spring late in a Red Wings victory, bringing the Joe Louis Arena fans to their feet, and he was looking for feedback.

"How was my form?" he asked. "Good?"

How did this start, one of the oddest traditions in sports? At playoff time in Detroit, fans throw octopi onto the ice. Sobotka, the Joe's manager who drives the Zamboni, picks them up and twirls them over his head in delight as the fans roar. Why? Who started this?

Pete Cusimano and his younger brother, Jerry, were working at the family market in Detroit in April 1952. They were excited about the Wings. In those days, you had to win two best-of-seven playoff series to win the Stanley Cup, and the Wings had swept the Toronto Maple Leafs and were working on sweeping the Montreal Canadiens. As they put some four-pound octopi on display, they got an idea.

An octopus has eight legs.

You needed eight victories to win the Cup.

Why not throw an octopus onto the ice as a good luck charm?

That night, they did. After the Wings' first goal of the game, they hurled an octopus from the lower bowl at Olympia Stadium. It hit near a faceoff circle and slid all the way to the near blue line.

A linesman skated over to take a look, went to pick it up—and recoiled. Defenseman Marcel Pronovost ended up whacking it away with his stick.

"Pronovost thought it was alive," Pete said. "But it was dead and cooked."

The Cusimano brothers didn't plan to do it again. No one knew they were the ones who had done it, and they could have gotten into trouble. But the Wings completed a sweep of the Canadiens—eight games, eight victories, eight legs, one Cup—and the next year the Detroit papers wondered if another octopus would be tossed.

So the Cusimanos did it again. And again. And again.

And a tradition was born.

Jerry died in a car accident in 1954, and Pete eventually stopped going to Wings games when his sons started playing hockey. But others kept the tradition alive.

Not everyone did it right. A raw octopus is really slimy, not to mention smelly. A boiled octopus is firm, its tentacles curl up, and it

Al Sobotka does more than drive the Zamboni at Joe Louis Arena. At playoff time, he picks octopi off the ice and twirls them to the delight of the roaring crowd.

By the NUMBERS

411—Consecutive sellouts at Joe Louis Arena through 2005–2006, regular season and playoffs combined. Owner Mike Ilitch went from giving away cars to get people into the building in the eighties to having a long waiting list for season tickets.

bounces. But—even if the NHL prohibited throwing objects, let alone seafood, onto the ice—it was all in good fun.

The Wings eventually adopted the octopus as an unofficial mascot, naming it Al for Sobotka, and put it on T-shirts, flags, you name it. They even made stuffed-animal octopi and hung a huge octopus with a mean scowl and blinking red eyes in the rafters for playoff games.

The Cusimano brothers became legends. They were even mentioned in the board game *Trivial Pursuit*. Pete carries the card laminated in his wallet.

"Q: What was the superfan Pete Cusimano famed for tossing onto the ice at Detroit Red Wings NHL games in the Olympia?

"A: Octopuses."

The Prison Game

The Red Wings once played an exhibition in a penalty box.

That's right. *In* a penalty box.

A penalty box called Marquette Prison.

Richard Bak told the story in *Detroit Red Wings: The Illustrated History*. General manager and coach Jack Adams was touring the joint one day in 1953, when he ran into a couple of inmates he had met before, gangsters Ray Bernstein and Harry Keywell, who used to hang around the Detroit sports scene. They asked him if he would bring in the Wings for a scrimmage someday.

Knowing full well the prison had no team and no rink, Adams said sure, no problem. He didn't give it another thought. Little did he know the warden was in the process of hiring Oakie Brumm, a former University of Michigan hockey player, as the prison athletic director. And little did he know the inmates would bug Brumm so much about the Wings coming that Brumm would put together a team and a rink.

Adams donated equipment from a defunct Wings farm club, Brumm drilled his inmates throughout the winter of 1953–1954, and Adams lived up to his promise. The semipro Marquette Sentinels sponsored the trip and chartered a DC-3, and the Wings made the trek to the Upper Peninsula of Michigan.

Now, the Wings were tough guys. But the prisoners were bad guys—murderers, thieves, the worst of the worst. How were they going to react to each other? The teams met on a manicured outdoor ice surface in the prison yard on the overcast, 21-degree afternoon of February 2, 1954.

The inmates surrounding the rink rooted for the Wings.

TOP TEN

Red Wings on Postseason All-Star Teams

		First team	Second team	Total
1.	Gordie Howe, RW	12	9	21
2.	Ted Lindsay, LW	8	1	9
3.	Red Kelly, D	6	2	8
4.	Nicklas Lidstrom, D	7	0	7†
	Terry Sawchuk, G	3	4	7†
6.	Jack Stewart, D	3	2	5
7.	Marcel Pronovost, D	2	2	4
8.	Sid Abel, C*	2	1	3
	Ebbie Goodfellow, D	2	1	3†
	Bill Quackenbush, D	2	1	3†
	Jack Adams, coach	2	1	3†

*Abel also made a second All-Star Team as a left wing

"Most of them were great hockey fans," forward Johnny Wilson said. "They listened to all the games on the radio. They knew the boys and were cheering us on, which was kind of nice."

The inmates on the rink were mesmerized by the Wings—Gordie Howe, Ted Lindsay, Red Kelly, Terry Sawchuk, and the rest of the crew in the midst of winning four Stanley Cups in six years.

"Howe would get the puck and circle the net three times before putting it in," Wilson said. "It was funny to watch."

After an 18–0 first period, they stopped keeping score. When the game was over, Brumm awarded Adams a "honey bucket," the kind of pail prisoners used in their cells as a toilet. Adams hoisted it high by the handle as his players looked on, smiling.

"This is a great day," Adams said. "I'm proud to have such a fine farm team up here in the north. The only

TRIVIA

Which Red Wing has not won the Lady Byng Memorial Trophy for sportsmanship, gentlemanly conduct, and a high standard of playing ability?

A. Marty Barry
B. Bill Quackenbush
C. Dutch Reibel
D. Nicklas Lidstrom

Answers to the trivia questions are on pages 185–186.

trouble is, you guys sure have made it tough for me to recruit any of you."

The Wings played an exhibition against the Sentinels that night, too, before flying back to Detroit the next day. Brumm played in both games, and one of the Wings, Jim Hay, was surprised to see him in the second one.

"He said, 'How in the hell did you get out to play down here tonight?'" Brumm said. "I guess throughout the entire afternoon he never realized I was working at the prison instead of doing time."

The Richard Riot

In March 1955 the Red Wings found themselves in the middle of one of the worst incidents of violence in sports history. But the cause of the whole brouhaha helped them win their seventh straight regular-season title and fourth Stanley Cup in six years.

These were the days when the Wings' Gordie Howe and the Montreal Canadiens' Maurice "Rocket" Richard were rivals. Everyone debated who was better, the best player in the game. Howe was a tough son of a gun—he could knock your teeth out just as easily as he could knock in a couple of goals—but he had much more control over his temper than the fiery Rocket did.

On March 13, in a game at the Boston Garden, Richard lost it and attacked linesman Cliff Thompson. NHL president Clarence Campbell suspended Richard for the rest of the regular season and the playoffs.

Montrealers, at least the French speakers, feeling this was the result of anti-French bias, were furious. Richard was leading the league in scoring, the Habs were clinging to a slim lead over the Wings, and the teams had a home-and-home series coming up.

On March 17 the Wings faced the Canadiens at the Forum, and Campbell was foolish enough to show up. The Wings took a 4–1 lead in the first period, and the fans gave Campbell a hard time, pelting him with garbage and insults. Then somebody attacked Campbell. Then a tear-gas bomb went off, and the Richard Riot was on.

The Wings hunkered down in the visitors' dressing room during the first intermission.

"We watered down some towels and pressed them into the crack of the door so none of the gas would come in," trainer Lefty Wilson said in Richard Bak's *Detroit Red Wings: The Illustrated History*.

The Red Wings and Canadiens had quite a rivalry in the 1950s. Metro Prystai struck a blow for Detroit against Gerry McNeil when the Wings won the 1952 Stanley Cup.

Eventually, Campbell came into the room with Montreal general manager Frank Selke, who had written a simple note to Detroit general manager Jack Adams, forfeiting the game.

"We were all surprised," said coach Jimmy Skinner in Rich Kincaide's *The Gods of Olympia Stadium: Legends of the Detroit Red Wings.* "And then Jack says, 'It's time to get out. Go out the back way.'"

It was bad. Someone shot out a Forum window. A mob made its way down Saint Catherine Street, looting stores, overturning cars, and battling police. When the Wings got on their train, several hooligans threatened to bring the disturbance to Detroit. It took a special radio appeal by the Rocket himself to restore order.

By the **NUMBERS** **100**—The career-goal milestone Gordie Howe reached February 17, 1951, against the Canadiens in Montreal on "Rocket Richard Day." Howe and Maurice "Rocket" Richard, No. 9 and No. 9, were constantly compared. The debate raged as to who was the greatest player.

With police in force in and around Olympia Stadium, nothing happened in the second game—nothing except a 6–0 victory for the Red Wings.

Richard ended up losing his scoring title to teammate Bernie "Boom Boom" Geoffrion by one point, and that was painful. Richard led the league in goals five times, but never led it in scoring.

The Habs ended up losing the regular-season title to the Wings by two points.

Then, in the playoffs, without Richard, the Habs lost the Cup Finals to the Wings in seven games. Howe, Richard's rival, set a new playoffs scoring record that year with 20 points.

TRIVIA

Who played goal for the Red Wings, Toronto Maple Leafs, and Boston Bruins— all while working for Detroit?

Answers to the trivia questions are on pages 185–186.

Close Call

When Dr. John Finley retired in 2003 after 46 years as the Red Wings' team physician—23 at Olympia Stadium, 23 at Joe Louis Arena—he had more than enough memories to fill a book.

Sure, there was medical drama. Finley had handled all sorts of situations, from helping Gordie Howe endure a kidney stone to taking out Steve Yzerman's tonsils. Ted Lindsay took at least three hundred stitches from Finley. When the Wings honored Finley's 40th anniversary with the team in April 1997, Lindsay appeared on the scoreboard screen at the Joe. He joked that he deserved some credit for Finley's skills.

"I donated my body," he said.

But that's not all. Finley remembers how the players used to drink tea with honey between periods (and how Lipton got wind of it and ran an ad in *Life* magazine showing the Wings' dressing room), how trainer Lefty Wilson got thrown out of a game for razzing a referee, how owner Bruce Norris wanted to start a European league, how coach Ned Harkness brought the Wings' training facilities into modernity, how coach and assistant general manager Nick Polano helped bring over Europeans.

There was the time his wife, Genevieve, went into labor during a game. One of the Finleys' guests had to take her to the hospital, because goaltender Roger Crozier had been hit in the head with a puck and the good doctor had to work. By the time he caught up with Genevieve, their sixth child and fifth daughter, Colleen, had been born.

There was the time he nearly had to see a doctor himself—the time he got shot at outside Olympia.

It was a cold January night in 1970, and the Wings had earned a rare victory over the powerful Chicago Black Hawks. About an hour

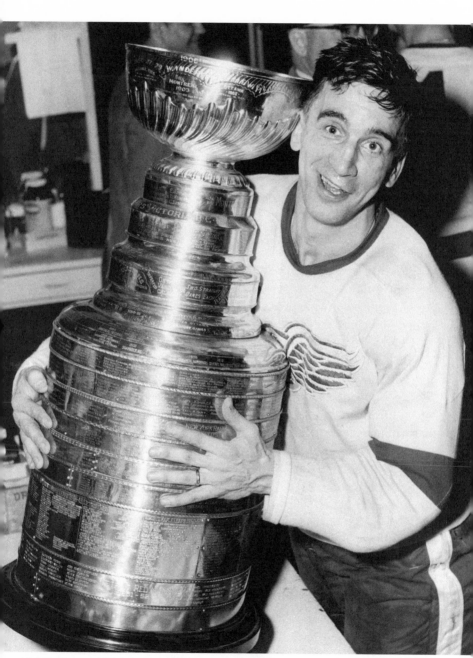

Ted Lindsay wouldn't look so good with the Stanley Cup if not for the steady hand of Dr. John Finley, who gave Lindsay at least 300 stitches during his playing career.

TRIVIA

What number did Gordie Howe wear with the Red Wings before donning the immortal No. 9?

A. 3
B. 4
C. 17
D. 99

Answers to the trivia questions are on pages 185–186.

after the game, Finley walked out the front door and headed to the back of the building to get his car. He was alone, it was dark, and he noticed two men approaching from behind, which made him nervous.

He snapped his fingers as if he had forgotten something and turned around to go back inside.

"One of them I could see had a pistol," Finley said. "He stuck it out and said, 'Turn around and keep walking.' I said, 'Not a chance.'"

According to a newspaper clipping Finley saved, he knocked aside the gun with a hand, and the gun went off.

"The bullet went through my car coat, went through my suit coat, tore the lining of my suit coat, and missed me completely," Finley said. He smiled. "Can you imagine that?"

The men took off, and Finley ducked into the building and found Genevieve.

"Did you just witness a shooting?" she asked.

"Yes," he said. "Stay in here."

As he ran out to Grand River looking for a police car, he didn't tell her he was the one who had been shot at.

"Here we had six little kids at the time," he said.

By the NUMBERS

5'8"—The height listed for Red Wings great Ted Lindsay, one of the most fearsome players in hockey history. He was known as "Terrible Ted" because of his mean streak. He was also known as "Scarface" because he had taken so many stitches.

The Odd Couple

Gordie Howe and Ted Lindsay weren't just part of the Production Line in the Red Wings' glory years of the fifties, they were best friends—until they had a falling-out in the seventies and stopped speaking to each other.

They had a lot of differences. That's what brought them together in the beginning and what helped tear them apart in the end.

Howe was big, 6', 205 pounds; Lindsay was small, 5'8", 163 pounds. Howe was quiet and shy; Lindsay was never afraid to speak his mind. The Wings roomed Howe with Lindsay hoping Lindsay would help Howe out of his shell. Howe lived with Lindsay for a while even after Lindsay got married.

The two seemed inseparable—on the ice, in the scoring rankings, off the ice. But Howe was the type of player to trust management and not push for as much money as he could get, while Lindsay clashed with management and tried to start an NHL players' association—getting himself traded to the Chicago Black Hawks because of it.

"It started with the players' association," said forward Marty Pavelich in Rich Kincaide's *The Gods of Olympia Stadium: Legends of the Detroit Red Wings*. "Then it just grew from there."

Howe and Lindsay talked about it in Kincaide's book.

"Ted was my best friend, but we drifted apart," Howe said. "Why? Well, we never did anything the same. He didn't like golf. He didn't like fishing. And some things happened between us."

After retiring from the Wings in 1971, Howe had come back and played four seasons with his sons, Mark and Marty, with the Houston Aeros of the World Hockey Association. But Howe wanted to play one

TRIVIA

What number did Ted Lindsay wear in his swan-song season with the Red Wings?

A. 7
B. 14
C. 15
D. 17

Answers to the trivia questions are on pages 185–186.

year with Mark and Marty in Detroit. (One year after Howe left the team, the Aeros folded.)

"The Red Wings weren't doing very well," Howe said. "In fact, they were terrible."

Lindsay was the Wings' general manager in 1977 and, according to Howe, said he didn't know if Mark could make it. The Howes spent two seasons with the New England Whalers of the WHA, then played a season with the Hartford Whalers in the NHL. Mark ended up becoming a star defenseman.

"He was another Red Kelly back there," Howe said. "People make mistakes."

Pictured below (left to right): Gordie Howe with Marcel Provonost, Sid Abel, and Val Fontaine.

By the NUMBERS **215**—Points produced by the Red Wings' Production Line of Ted Lindsay, Sid Abel, and Gordie Howe in 1949–1950, when the trio went 1–2–3 in NHL scoring. Lindsay, the left wing, had 23 goals and 55 assists for 78 points. Abel, the center, had 34 goals and 35 assists for 69 points. Howe, the right wing, had 35 goals and 33 assists for 68 points.

But that wasn't all. Howe said Lindsay made a comment about his wife, Colleen, a strong-willed woman who handled her husband's business affairs.

"I don't know why in the hell Colleen got to him, but he said, 'I wouldn't want her running into my office all year,'" Howe said. "So that was that. Nobody picks on your family. Who the hell needs that?"

Lindsay didn't go into detail.

"We had a pretty good thing going at one time, Gordie and I," he said. "Sure we did. Certainly we were close; we *were* that. But it's happened before in sports, and I guess it will happen again. . . .

"I doubt Gordie and I talking again will ever happen. But who knows what will happen? I don't dwell on that subject. There are many, many things that are mine and will stay with me, and that are nobody's business. And nobody will know. To the grave, that's where it's going to go."

Great Escape

Sergei Fedorov was a walking soap opera when he played for the Red Wings from 1990 to 2003. The controversies over his performance on the ice were the least of it. From his contract disputes to his Ferraris to his friend/girlfriend/wife/ex-wife Anna Kournikova, the tennis sex symbol, he was always a story.

Fitting, then, that his days in Detroit began like something out of a spy novel.

Fedorov was born in Pskov, outside what is now St. Petersburg, Russia. He grew up in Apatiti, a town above the Arctic Circle. He skated on a frozen river and played wing on an adult hockey team, with his father, Viktor, at center. He was on the ice as much as four or five hours a day. At age 13 he went to a special sports school in Minsk, in what is now Belarus. From there he went to the Red Army and the national team.

This is where he became an elite talent. His father made him drill— jumping up from his knees on the ice, jumping up the stairs to his family's fifth-floor apartment—to build leg muscles and encourage quickness. His coaches made him play different positions to develop his all-around skills.

But this was also the Soviet Union. The Iron Curtain had not yet lifted, and that meant the Russians weren't allowing their hockey players to go to North America. So when Fedorov was a 20-year-old draft pick ready for the NHL, he had to sneak away.

The Wings helped Fedorov defect while he was playing at a tournament in Portland, Oregon. His team was staying at a Holiday Inn on the outskirts of the city. On his way to a game, Fedorov discreetly dropped his room key in the lobby so a Wings official could enter his room and gather his belongings.

"He had a little bag with hardly anything in it," said Nick Polano, the Wings' assistant general manager at the time and the plan's mastermind.

On his way back from the game, Fedorov spotted a man reading a newspaper—it was a signal—and followed him out a back door. They ducked into a waiting limousine, drove to the airport, and dashed into a waiting airplane—Wings owner Mike Ilitch's private jet.

"We were back in Detroit before they [the Soviets] even knew he was gone," Polano said.

The joy Sergei Fedorov feels when he scores a goal is nothing compared to the emotion he felt when he defected from the Soviet Union.

IF ONLY . . . Sergei Fedorov had been a defenseman, he might have been one of the best in the NHL, a perennial candidate for the Norris Trophy. That's what some scouts think. Red Wings coach Scotty Bowman put Fedorov on the blue line more than once. He did it to make a point, but also because Fedorov had the ability. Fedorov won the Selke Trophy as the NHL's best defensive forward twice.

Years later, after winning a Hart Memorial Trophy as the NHL's most valuable player, after twice winning the Selke Trophy as the league's best defensive forward, after winning the Stanley Cup three times, after making millions upon millions of dollars and living the good life of a North American professional athlete, Fedorov couldn't believe he had made it.

"I'm afraid sometimes to think about it," he said. "I've got chills going down my spine."

TOP TEN **Red Wings in the All-Star Game**

	Name	Games
1.	Gordie Howe*	22
2.	Alex Delvecchio*	13
3.	Ted Lindsay*	10†
	Steve Yzerman**	10†
5.	Red Kelly*	9†
	Marcel Pronovost*	9†
7.	Nicklas Lidstrom	8†
	Norm Ullman*	8†
9.	Sergei Fedorov	6
10.	John Ogrodnick	5†
	Brendan Shanahan	5†

*Played as member of Stanley Cup champions in 1950, 1954, or 1955

**Did not play in 1999 because of injury

The Great Outdoors

Ken Holland was the general manager of the Red Wings' 1998 and 2002 Stanley Cup teams. Bringing Dominik Hasek, Luc Robitaille, and Brett Hull to Detroit in the same summer, giving the Wings nine potential Hall of Famers in 2001–2002—that was Mr. Holland's opus.

But it was a long journey to that prominent position, one that took him to a bizarre rink in the middle of nowhere, to a game that seemed to be played in a time warp.

Holland was a humble goaltender. He played four NHL games, one with the Hartford Whalers in 1980–1981, three with the Wings in 1983–1984. But he went 0–2–1 with a 4.95 goals-against average, and he spent most of his nine-year professional career in the minor leagues. After he finished up in 1984–1985 with the Wings' American Hockey League affiliate in Glens Falls, New York, the Adirondack Red Wings, he was offered a chance to become the Wings' western Canada scout.

"The opportunity to remain in the game and have a job in the game after my playing days were over was something I never thought about," Holland said. "But when the opportunity presented itself, I jumped."

Holland, who was from Vernon, British Columbia, set up shop in Medicine Hat, Alberta, where he had played in juniors. The GM was already starting to come out in him. He had loved ball hockey as a kid, running in shoes, wearing shin pads, using a hockey stick to bat around a bounceless orange ball on a rink without ice. He started a summer rec league, ran a team, and called it the Red Wings.

In the midnineties, now the real Wings' chief amateur scout, he took a trip to Russia. One of the Wings' scouts wanted him to see a certain player, so they drove three hours from Moscow to a small town. The

Brett Hull joined Scotty Bowman and the Red Wings as a free agent in 2001. Ken Holland landed Dominik Hasek and Luc Robitaille earlier that off-season.

game was supposed to be at noon, but when they got there at about 11:00 AM, the parking lot was empty.

Eight inches of snow. No tire tracks.

"I thought we were in the wrong place," Holland said.

But there was a sign on the door that said, "Game at noon today," so they opened the door and went in. They found the player and met him, then grabbed a bite to eat.

Noon rolled around.

"I assumed I was going to go into a covered rink," Holland said, "and we walked out through this door—and we were outside."

There was a sheet of ice. On one side, there were frigid concrete steps for stands. On the other, snow was stacked about 10 or 12 feet high. There were maybe 800 or 900 people there.

"Both teams lined up on the blue line," Holland said. "They had the anthem, and then they got ready to drop the puck. The referee forgot the puck. There was a bit of confusion as they were searching for a puck. They found a puck. They dropped the puck.

"First shift of the game, a guy came around behind the net and shot the puck over the boards and into the bank of snow. So now there was more confusion. Finally, one of the players had to hop over the boards and dig around in the snow. He found the puck.

"As the night wore on, every time the puck went into the bank over there, someone went over the boards. And this was a professional league. . . . I thought it was the thirties. It was unbelievable."

And how was the player they had come all that way to see?

"He wasn't very good that night, I don't think," Holland said. "We didn't draft him."

10—Men who have held the title of general manager of the Red Wings:

Name	Years
Art Duncan	1926–1927
Jack Adams	1927–1928 to 1962–1963
Sid Abel	1963–1964 to 1970–1971
Ned Harkness	1970–1971 to 1973–1974
Alex Delvecchio	1974–1975 to 1976–1977
Ted Lindsay	1976–1977 to 1979–1980
Jimmy Skinner	1980–1981 to 1981–1982
Jimmy Devellano	1982–1983 to 1989–1990
Bryan Murray	1990–1991 to 1993–1994
Ken Holland	1997–1998 to 2005–2006

The Archrival Avalanche

Colorado. Claude Lemieux. No team and no player was more despised in Detroit in the late nineties. A costly loss, a cheap shot, and Red Wings–Avalanche, in the words of tough guy Darren McCarty, quickly became "one of the premier rivalries in sports."

The Wings were the odds-on favorites to win the 1996 Stanley Cup. They had made the finals the year before, and although they were swept by the New Jersey Devils, they had followed that up with a record 62 regular-season victories. This was supposed to be their year. They were supposed to be champions for the first time since 1955.

But in the Western Conference finals, the Wings met this new team, the Avs, who had been the Nordiques before moving from Quebec to Denver that season. The Wings lost in six games, a stunning upset.

And that wasn't the worst of it.

In Game 3 Lemieux sucker punched Wings forward Slava Kozlov, opening a 10-stitch cut, in retaliation for a hit Kozlov had put on defenseman Adam Foote. Detroit coach Scotty Bowman asked the NHL to review the incident, and Lemieux was suspended for a game. Colorado coach Marc Crawford was so angry, he said, "[Bowman] thinks so much, the plate in his head causes interference in our headsets."

In Game 6 Lemieux hit Wings center Kris Draper from behind into the boards in front of the Detroit bench. Draper suffered a broken jaw and nose, displaced teeth, and a concussion. He needed 30 stitches to mend his mouth. He would drink his meals from a straw for more than two weeks and lose 10 pounds because of it.

Lemieux received a five-minute penalty and an ejection, but he participated in the postgame handshakes. And in the aftermath, the Wings were appalled.

"I can't believe I shook his [bleeping] hand," Wings forward Dino Ciccarelli said, in a quote that became legendary. "I hadn't seen Kris's face. It's BS. Kris was one of our best players, and Lemieux blindsided him. The poor kid was right by the door, he had his back to him, he didn't have a chance. He was at his mercy. Lemieux could have broken his neck. Hey, they beat us, they had the better team—but that's just BS.

"I probably would have speared him in the face."

Lemieux was suspended for Colorado's first two games in the finals, but the Wings weren't satisfied.

Not even close.

"It makes me sick," said goaltender Chris Osgood, Draper's best friend and roommate, in the *Detroit Free Press*. "He has done it too many times, and I'll say it now: a suspension is not good enough for him anymore. When he comes back to play the Red Wings next year, we'll be waiting for him. And he'd better be ready.

Martin Lapointe versus Eric Lacroix and Brendan Shanahan versus Rene Corbet: just two skirmishes in the Detroit-Colorado war of the late 1990s.

"He can say what he wants about going to the finals. We know we're not going. We can deal with our situation. He'd better be ready to deal with what he's going to have to face next season. It's not a threat. It's just something that's going to happen."

Lemieux missed the first two games between the teams in 1996–1997. He escaped the third game unscathed.

Then came the fourth game: Fight Night at the Joe.

During a scrum late in the first period, McCarty spun off a linesman and started pummeling Lemieux. As the fans rose to their feet, Lemieux assumed the turtle position. McCarty held Lemieux by the back of the neck with one hand and smacked him with the other. He wasn't finished until he dragged Lemieux's bloody body in front of the Detroit bench—in front of Draper.

"I guess it was payback," McCarty said in the *Free Press*. "An opportunity presented itself, and something happened."

All hell broke loose. While McCarty was beating up Lemieux, Colorado goaltender Patrick Roy left his crease, and Wings forward Brendan Shanahan came flying in to intercept him.

"I don't know what to say about that," Shanahan said in the *Free Press*. "There was a little WWF from both of us there. I saw Patrick going for McCarty, and I didn't want him to sneak up on him, so I went after him.

"When I was three feet in the air, I was thinking, 'What am I doing?' When I was five feet in the air, I said, 'What am I really doing here?'"

The fight-filled game lasted three and a half hours. Wings goaltender Mike Vernon, all 5'9" of him, even took on Roy, a six-footer. The Wings won it in overtime, 6–5, on a goal by—who else?—McCarty.

The Avs were incensed afterward. Crawford even elbowed Wings defenseman Aaron Ward and tried to barge into the officials' dressing room.

By the NUMBERS **62**—Wins the Red Wings recorded in 1995–1996, an NHL record. The 131 points they racked up that season rank second only to Montreal's 132 in 1976–1977. Scotty Bowman coached both of those teams.

"I think that team has no heart," Colorado forward Mike Keane said, in another quote that became legendary. "Detroit had the opportunity to do that in our building, but they didn't.... I think they showed their true colors tonight. Everyone is gutless on that team, and I'd love to see them in the playoffs."

Keane should have been careful what he wished for. He saw them in the playoffs all right, and Game 4 of the Western Conference finals became Fight Night II. While Fight Night I featured 148 penalty minutes, this one featured 236—and 204 of them came in the third period.

With 2:18 left, Crawford climbed the glass separating the teams' benches and screamed at Bowman—who basically laughed. Bowman knew Crawford's father, Floyd, from junior hockey.

"I knew your father before you did, and I don't think he'd be too proud of what you're doing right now," Bowman told him.

The Wings won the game, 6–0, and went on to win the series in six. Afterward, Draper refused to shake Lemieux's hand, because Lemieux wouldn't make eye contact with him, and Lemieux refused to shake McCarty's.

"Obviously," Draper said in the *Free Press*, "there's a lot of bad blood between these two hockey clubs."

The bad blood—and the great hockey—would keep bubbling for years to come.

As Wings center Sergei Fedorov said so well, "It's important to focus when you play Colorado. Otherwise ... [smile] ... you might get smashed into the boards."

One day, Draper laughed about it.

"Lucky me," he said. "I got to have my face rearranged to start a rivalry."

TRIVIA

True or false: Joe Kocur was a member of the Grind Line, the checking line that was enormously popular with the blue-collar Detroit fans from 1996–1997 to 2003–2004.

Answers to the trivia questions are on pages 185–186.

Hockeytown

First, Detroit was the Motor City. Then, it was Motown. And then, as the Red Wings returned to glory in the nineties, it became Hockeytown.

The word was painted in big, black, arrogant letters across center ice at Joe Louis Arena. It was displayed on bold banners that hung from lampposts along Jefferson Avenue. It was everywhere. It was just a marketing concept at first, but it grew into another alternate identity for the area, something Wings fans could rally around and boast about.

The *Detroit Free Press* reported how it all started: one summer Gary Topolewski was given two weeks or so to come up with an advertising campaign for the Wings, something to fill a few billboards, and his team at Bozell Worldwide in suburban Detroit threw out "Hockeytown" in a brainstorming session.

"I just pointed to the wall and said, 'That's it, right there,'" Topolewski said. "We just kind of knew. There was no debate. It popped out at me as soon as we thought of it."

There were reservations. Everyone knew that people from Toronto to Montreal to Moscow would beg to differ, pointing out that they lived and died with the sport, not just the local team when it was successful. Hockeytown? People in Sault Ste. Marie, Michigan, said they came up with the concept first.

"I remember it being a hard sell," said John Van Osdol, who worked with Topolewski. The Wings "wanted to make sure they could hold up to that claim. That was their initial reluctance. 'Can we support that claim?' They weren't sure about this. They wanted to like it. They just weren't sure."

But the Wings went for it, and the Detroit area went for it, too, especially after the Wings ended a 42-year championship drought by winning

Thousands of fans descended on downtown Detroit's Hart Plaza after the Red Wings won the Stanley Cup in 1998. They did the same in 1997 and 2002.

By the NUMBERS **.614**—The Red Wings' regular-season winning percentage in the nineties, best in the NHL. They went 431–252–100. The New Jersey Devils were second with .578 (396–275–110), and the Pittsburgh Penguins were third at .577 (406–286–90).

the Stanley Cup in 1997. It caught on like a catchy tune, and it *was* a catchy tune. "Hey, hey, Hockeytown!" was played at the Joe.

The NHL asked the Wings if other teams could use Hockeytown, and the Wings refused. Other people mimicked it. A beer company created an ad campaign using "Hockey Falls." Minnesota called itself the "State of Hockey."

"I'll be honest with you," Topolewski said. "It amazes me because I'll see a Hockeytown logo on a car, and I remember distinctly looking at that, designing that. It's one of those special moments beyond marketing. It's really unbelievable."

It became a brand name. Owner Mike Ilitch built a restaurant on Woodward Avenue, next to the Fox Theatre, across from Comerica Park, not exactly near the Joe, and called it the Hockeytown Café. The Hockeytown logo was huge on the side of the building in the heart of Detroit's entertainment district.

"When I saw that go up, I went, 'Man, this is something else. There it is in lights,'" Topolewski said. "We were all excited about Hockeytown because it was so simple. Anything you have that really is true is simplicity. It's right under your nose—the purity of it, what it meant, the authenticity of it. It was very true."

Believe

Three days after the Red Wings won the 1997 Stanley Cup, one million fans jammed Woodward Avenue in downtown Detroit for a victory parade. Hockeytown had waited 42 years for a championship. It was time to celebrate.

People lined the entire route from the Fox Theatre to Hart Plaza. They held signs offering everything from congratulations to marriage proposals. They lifted replica Cups. They climbed trees, light poles, ladders, statues—whatever they could to get a better view of the players riding by in red Mustang convertibles.

"We expected a lot of people here," captain Steve Yzerman told the crowd at a rally. "We didn't expect this. I thought nothing would top Saturday night, but coming down Woodward was the best of all. It was the icing on the cake."

But three days later, on that same street, a few miles north in the suburbs, the celebration stopped. The story was chronicled in the *Detroit Free Press*.

Defenseman Vladimir Konstantinov and team masseur Sergei Mnatsakanov were critically injured in a limousine accident. Defenseman Slava Fetisov was in the car, too, but he was lucky. He suffered only a chest injury, a bruised lung, and a lifetime of haunting memories.

The crash occurred about 9:00 PM. Owner Mike Ilitch heard the news on television and rushed to the hospital, arriving around 10:45, dressed in a team windbreaker. Yzerman, Brendan Shanahan, Sergei Fedorov, Doug Brown, Martin Lapointe—almost the whole team followed.

Most of the players had been at a golf outing. Konstantinov, Mnatsakanov, and Fetisov had left early. Everyone was supposed to meet

When the Red Wings won the 1998 Stanley Cup, the first person captain Steve Yzerman handed the trophy to was injured defenseman Vladimir Konstantinov.

at Chris Osgood's house for a final victory party. Instead, they met in an intensive-care ward. As Mathieu Dandenault said: "It was the worst feeling ever."

Later, news came that the accident could have been avoided. Fetisov said the driver, Richard Gnida, appeared to fall asleep at the wheel. The passengers screamed and yelled, trying to wake him, but he didn't respond. The car crossed two lanes of traffic, jumped the curb, and hit a tree. Gnida received jail time and community service.

Konstantinov and Mnatsakanov suffered severe brain injuries. At first they responded to some stimuli—Russian music, kind words from teammates—but their improvement was slow and mild. Both remained in wheelchairs and struggled to speak.

TRIVIA

What two numbers aren't retired but are held out of circulation by the Red Wings—and out of respect for whom?

Answers to the trivia questions are on pages 185–186.

When Fetisov, Igor Larionov, and Slava Kozlov brought the Cup to Russia for the first time in history, Konstantinov and Mnatsakanov were unable to go with them.

"We talked about it a lot after we won the Cup," Fetisov said. "Vladdie had never been back to Russia since he left, and he was so excited about coming back."

The morning of the 1997–1998 home opener, Konstantinov and Mnatsakanov drank out of the Cup in the hospital. (Mnatsakanov asked for vodka, but all they got was juice.) That night, Irina Konstantinov and Ylena Mnatsakanov represented their husbands in the banner-raising ceremony.

"When their wives come to the ice, I think about Sergei and Vladdie very much, and I start to cry a little bit," Kozlov said. "We missed them very much."

The Wings had Konstantinov and Mnatsakanov on their minds constantly. All season they wore a special patch that had the word "believe" written in English and Russian. Konstantinov's locker was kept as if he would rejoin the lineup at any moment.

There were hospital visits. There was a visit to a Florida rehabilitation center during the All-Star break, when Konstantinov was able to support his weight and take a few steps with assistance. There was the visit to the White House, when Konstantinov joined them to meet President Clinton.

Coach Scotty Bowman often reminded his players of their priorities.

"Scotty told us to give our maximum effort for them," Lapointe said. "Scotty said that he would give up all of his Stanley Cup championship rings if the two of them could be standing with us in this locker room today. It was pretty inspiring."

When the Wings made the Western Conference finals, Konstantinov and Mnatsakanov returned to Joe Louis Arena. The Joe's DJ played "Bad to the Bone"—the Vladinator's, as Konstantinov was called, old theme song—and everyone looked up to Ilitch's private box. There they were.

"Vlad-die!" the fans chanted for a good two minutes. "Vlad-die!"

The players tapped their sticks on the ice—both the Wings and their opponents, the Dallas Stars.

"I saw him when everybody stand up, and I'm almost crying," Kozlov said. "I appreciate that people still love Vladdie and Sergei. It's a great feeling to see them here. I have incredible feeling right now."

TOP TEN

Red Wings Playoff Scoring Leaders

		GP	G	A	Pts.
1.	Steve Yzerman	196	70	115	185
2.	Sergei Fedorov	162	50	113	163
3.	Gordie Howe	154	67	91	158
4.	Nicklas Lidstrom	174	35	83	118
5.	Alex Delvecchio	121	35	69	104
6.	Ted Lindsay	123	44	44	88
7.	Vyacheslav Kozlov	114	42	37	79
8.	Norm Ullman	80	27	47	74
9.	Brendan Shanahan	106	33	41	74
10.	Igor Larionov	105	20	39	59

No one had a harder time with his emotions than Fetisov.

"If not for an inch," he said, "maybe it is me up there in that box and not on the ice. . . . I wake up in the night sometimes, I see the pictures in my head, but I cannot find an answer. Why this happen to Vladimir and Sergei and did not happen to me too?"

When the Wings won the Stanley Cup for the second straight year, Konstantinov was there. He sat in section 116 at Washington's MCI Center—appropriate, considering he wore No. 16 with the Wings—in front of a banner that said, "We Believe, You Believe."

With about eight and a half minutes to go in the game, he was wheeled down to the lower level, and when the Wings' sweep of the Capitals was complete, he was wheeled onto the ice. The Wings rushed to meet him. He clenched a cigar into his mouth, raised his index finger, and put on a 1998 Stanley Cup champions cap.

Yzerman raised the Cup, then put it on Konstantinov's lap. Everyone gathered around for a group photo.

"This," Larionov said, "is Vladdie's Cup."

TRIVIA

Which one of these Red Wings was not one of the Russian Five?

A. Slava Fetisov
B. Slava Kozlov
C. Igor Larionov
D. Pavel Datsyuk

Answers to the trivia questions are on pages 185–186.

Making History

The Red Wings had so many accomplished players in the late 1990s and early 2000s, it seemed someone was always reaching a milestone or setting a record. Making history was so routine it sometimes went overlooked at the time.

These are some of the most interesting or important stories.

Steve Yzerman's 600th goal, November 26, 1999

Yzerman picked up a loose puck low in the faceoff circle to the right of Edmonton Oilers goaltender Tommy Salo, on the power play, midway through the first period. He circled. He took a couple of purposeful strides behind the goal line, heading toward the net, eyes up, searching unselfishly for a teammate with a better angle to shoot.

And he found one.

So Yzerman, 12:30 into his 1,201st NHL game, leading his team in his 14th campaign as the Captain, looking as much like a Hall of Famer as ever in his 17th season as a Wing, flipped a pass for teammate Slava Kozlov.

But instead of flying across the crease and onto Kozlov's tape, the puck struck Salo's glove, squirted off Salo's left skate, and suddenly scooted into history. Salo's head drooped.

Score. Sweet 600.

Stunned and surprised, Joe Louis Arena erupted in applause and outright, unabashed noise. Yzerman, who insisted for more than a week that he found little meaning in becoming only the 11th player in history to score 600 career goals, glided behind the net with his arms by his side, stone-faced, because he had more than two-thirds of a game left to play.

Martin Lapointe and Steve Duchesne met him near the boards for a hug and a head rub. Kozlov and Nicklas Lidstrom arrived on the scene a second later. Yzerman skated over to the Wings' bench, using his right index finger to push his helmet up off his brow. He was still stone-faced, but no matter how hard he tried to concentrate on the task at hand, he soon couldn't help himself.

As the crowd kept up its crazy thumping and cheering, Yzerman saw his teammates, all leaning over the boards, smiling, gloves extended for fist-bumps. The corners of his mouth began to rise. By the time Yzerman reached the end of the receiving line, he was flashing a full-fledged smile.

Soon afterward, answering thunderous appeals from the 19,983 fans, Yzerman stood in the bench area, punched his right arm into the air, and raised his stick, thanking those who were thanking him.

"I just picked up a loose puck," Yzerman said. "I was looking for Kozzie, the goalie reached out to block the pass, and it redirected in off his glove. I don't know if I deserved it, but I'm taking it. . . .

"Ideally, I would have drawn it up a little prettier than that. But I've gotten some lousy goals over the years, too."

The goal made Yzerman only the fifth player to record 600 goals and 900 assists, joining the exclusive fraternity of Wayne Gretzky, Gordie Howe, Marcel Dionne, and Mark Messier.

It provided additional evidence that Yzerman was nothing but a gem.

"If you're a miner and you find a diamond . . . well, a lot of people find diamonds," associate coach Dave Lewis said. "But when you find a large one, that's pretty impressive. That's pretty rare. That's sort of the way I look at it: he's a rare individual."

Yzerman said scoring 600 wasn't really a big deal, even if it confirmed his status as one of the sport's all-time greats.

"I don't really use that as a barometer," Yzerman said. "I just kind of play. That's a total of the last 17 years, and it doesn't really matter at this point. I just worry about playing now. I really don't think about it. It's not like you sit there and really are aware of it."

Yzerman said that although he always had been an eager student of hockey history, he had never visited the Hall of Fame.

"One day, I want to go," he said.

The Hall is waiting.

Larry Murphy's 1,200ᵗʰ point, November 1, 2000

When Doug Brown scored 6:51 into the second period against the Montreal Canadiens, defenseman Larry Murphy celebrated. The goal, not his assist. Although the point was his 1,200th in the NHL, Murphy didn't pick up the puck.

"I wish I had," Murphy said. "I just forgot about it."

The souvenir would have been significant. To put 1,200 points in perspective, consider that, at the time, only 30 players had recorded that many and only three of them were defensemen. Paul Coffey and Ray Bourque were the others.

"I guess I'll just have to get 1,300," Murphy said at the time.

Murphy finished his NHL career with 1,216. He retired in 2001 and was inducted into the Hall of Fame in 2004.

Luc Robitaille's 611ᵗʰ goal, January 18, 2002

One minute, 50 seconds into a game against the Washington Capitals, Robitaille broke Bobby Hull's record for goals by an NHL left wing.

Kirk Maltby fired a shot from the left point. Just off the left pad of goaltender Olaf Kolzig, just in front of defenseman Brendan Witt, his skates in the crease, Robitaille stuck out his stick and deflected the puck.

And scored number 611.

"A typical goal by me," Robitaille said. "I just tipped it into the net."

A few minutes later, public address announcer Budd Lynch acknowledged the feat. Players on both sides tapped their sticks against the boards and ice. The fans gave a standing ovation, underscoring it with what had become a common cry of Joe Louis Arena jubilation, a deep-throated "LUUUC!"

Sitting in section 212A, row 12, seat 2, was Hull.

"That certainly makes it pretty special," Robitaille said. "It's going to be meaningful once I retire, but I don't want to stop here. I want to keep going and win a Cup."

The Capitals responded. But the Wings took a 2–1 lead with 46 seconds left in the first period, and the man who scored was . . .

Hull's son, Brett.

And as it turned out, the goal was the game winner. Brett's 99th game winner, putting him past Bobby into third on the all-time list, just behind Gordie Howe (121) and Phil Esposito (118).

Larry Murphy wasn't a quick skater, but he was a quick thinker, and that helped him to amass more than 1,200 NHL points.

Sergei Fedorov scored 6:25 into the third, securing the victory, so with about two minutes still remaining, Bobby was safe to leave his seat and head down the steps. When the surrounding fans began to cheer, Bobby smiled and held a forefinger to his lips, as if to say, "Shhh . . ." It wasn't his night.

He made his way down to the dressing room.

"What are records for?" he asked.

"To be broken," a reporter said.

"Thank you," he said.

Robitaille asked Bobby to pose for a picture. He told him his first pair of skates was a Bobby Hull CCM model. Robitaille, in a sweaty gray T-shirt, clenched a cigar in his smile and the puck in his hand, "611" written in black marker on white tape stuck to the rubber. Bobby, in a dark overcoat, held Robitaille's "610" puck.

Bobby gave Robitaille that cigar—and laughed because Brett had given it to him for Christmas.

"So if Luc gets the cigar," a reporter asked, "what's Brett get?"

"Well," Bobby said, "he gets my love."

Brett Hull's 732nd goal, December 8, 2003

Hull beamed like a little boy. He had scored in overtime, and the goal was his 732nd, putting him past Marcel Dionne into third place on the NHL's all-time list, behind only Wayne Gretzky (894) and Gordie Howe (801).

"I can't put it into words what it means," he said, "because one guy is known as the greatest player ever and the other guy is known as Mr. Hockey."

"And what are you known as?" he was asked.

"I don't know," he said, laughing. "Kind of the pain in the ass of hockey."

He laughed some more.

"I mean, two out of three ain't bad," he said. "I know it's an honor to be there, I'll tell you that. With the likes of them, it's special."

Hull hardly could have reached the milestone in a better way. It wasn't just that he gave the Wings an overtime victory at home. He did it in vintage Brett Hull style, dropping to his right knee and one-timing a cross-ice feed from Mathieu Schneider.

As Hull waited to do a TV interview outside the dressing room after the game, Howe came up and congratulated him. Hull said the only person who would have moved him more at that moment would have been his father. Howe said he was happy the goal meant so much to Hull.

TRIVIA

On which holiday(s) do the Red Wings have a winning record?

A. Halloween

B. New Year's Eve

C. Valentine's Day

D. St. Patrick's Day

Answers to the trivia questions are on pages 185–186.

"When he scores, his arms generally don't go up," Howe said. "But he was pretty darn happy, which is good."

Hull made his way into the room, sat in front of his stall, peeled off the top half of his equipment, tried to express his feelings—and failed.

"I'm dumbfounded," he said. "I'm not at a loss for words very often, but I don't know how to explain it. I just wanted one day to play in the league, give it a shot, see what I could do. To have it come to this point . . . I don't know how to explain it. It's hard to talk when you're shivering because of the goose bumps."

Eventually, he came up with a good explanation.

"From Adam Oates to Wayne Gretzky to Mike Modano to Pavel Datsyuk, I've had a chance to play with some of the greatest centermen and greatest players," he said. "I've been lucky enough to be smart enough to play within the system yet figure out a way to go to places and score goals. It's all the people that I've played with. If Schneider doesn't give me a great pass there, it's no goal. It's everybody that's helped me. I was blessed with a great shot, and that's helped."

After some more interviews, Hull took a picture with the puck, the stick, and the teammates who assisted on the goal, Schneider and Jason Woolley.

"He's just incredible," Schneider said. "He continues to score at a tremendous pace. Nowadays, when there's not an awful lot of scoring in the league, he seems to keep doing it."

Steve Yzerman's 1,024ᵗʰ assist, January 5, 2004

No one picked up the puck. No announcement was made.

No one noticed.

By the
NUMBERS

50—Number of NHL arenas, not including neutral sites, in which defenseman Larry Murphy played before he retired as a Red Wing in 2001. Murphy played 21 seasons in the league, going from Los Angeles to Washington to Minnesota (North Stars) to Pittsburgh to Toronto and finally to Detroit.

But when Kris Draper scored in a rout of the Nashville Predators, Yzerman had earned his 1,024[th] assist—breaking Gordie Howe's team record.

Even Yzerman had no idea until he was told the next day.

"I guess I'm a little surprised," he said. "I didn't expect to catch him on any lists."

The Captain was unlikely to catch Mr. Hockey on any more of the team scoring lists—Yzerman had 672 goals and 1,697 points, while Howe had 786 and 1,809 as a Red Wing—but that made this accomplishment all the more meaningful.

"Gordie is the greatest Red Wing ever," coach Dave Lewis said, "and for Stevie to pass him is just phenomenal."

Yzerman played down the accomplishment, as he usually played down records and milestones, saying he really never concerned himself with such things too much and concerned himself with them even less now.

"It doesn't matter to me where I sit on any lists," he said.

But he said he would have been happy to keep the puck, had someone grabbed it for him.

And he was able to keep the puck, after all. The Wings collected pucks that had been used to score goals—so they could sell them, give them to charity, or give them to the players—and they fished this one out for him.

Faceoff

No one takes injuries in stride like hockey players. Consider what happened with Red Wings forward Darren McCarty on October 13, 1999.

In the second period of a game against St. Louis, McCarty was battling for a puck behind the Blues' net when, in a tangle of bodies, one of teammate Yuri Butsayev's skates clipped him near his left eye. He felt the cut. He knew he was bleeding. But he didn't think it was serious.

He skated over to the Detroit bench and reluctantly saw trainer John Wharton.

"Put something on it so I can finish the period."

Wharton looked at the cut. His face went white.

"Um," he said, "no."

Little did McCarty know his face was missing a nickel-sized piece of flesh.

A group of Wings searched the ice, and center Sergei Fedorov made a discovery in one of the, ahem, faceoff circles.

"I find it," Fedorov said. "I find his skin. At first I passed by it, because I didn't know it was one of ours, but then I go back."

Said forward Martin Lapointe, "There was a piece of hair sticking out, and we said, 'Well, that must be Darren's eyebrow.'"

Fedorov and forward Brendan Shanahan used their sticks to scoop up the skin and take it to the bench resting on some snow. You might say they helped McCarty save face, or that they saved his skin.

"It was a chunk," Wharton said. "It looked like a chunk of salmon. Some of the guys were grossed out on the bench."

As team physician John Finley used about 40 stitches to reattach the chunk, forward Stacy Roest, a healthy scratch, called McCarty's wife,

TOP TEN

Red Wings Scoring Leaders

		GP	G	A	Pts.
1.	Gordie Howe	1,687	786	1,023	1,809
2.	Steve Yzerman	1,514	692	1,063	1,755
3.	Alex Delvecchio	1,549	456	825	1,281
4.	Sergei Fedorov	908	400	554	954
5.	Nicklas Lidstrom	1,096	189	617	807
6.	Norm Ullman	875	324	434	758
7.	Ted Lindsay	862	335	393	728
8.	Brendan Shanahan	716	309	324	633
9.	Reed Larson	708	188	382	570
10.	John Ogrodnick	558	265	281	546

Cheryl, to let her know everything was fine. She wasn't worried. After all, she had seen her husband's forearm slashed by a skate, his hand run over by a skate—and much, much more.

"She's seen a lot of injuries," McCarty said. "It's just another one to go into the weird-injury category."

When Finley was finished, McCarty looked a little like Frankenstein's monster. Forward Kris Draper, one of McCarty's close friends, kidded him by saying, "It looks like an anchovy." But in hockey terms, McCarty was fine.

"It looks pretty good," Lapointe said.

TRIVIA

Who were known as the Bruise Brothers in the eighties?

A. Lee Norwood and Gilbert Delorme
B. Lee Norwood and Bob Probert
C. Bob Probert and Joe Kocur
D. Joe Kocur and Darren McCarty

Answers to the trivia questions are on pages 185–186.

Now, McCarty could have been blinded.

"When I looked in the mirror, I realized how serious it was," he said. "It's close to my eye. It's a game of inches, right? I have to thank my lucky stars."

But when he came back and played nearly four minutes in the third period, he griped all the while about having to wear a face shield.

"It stinks," he said. "I hated wearing one in juniors. It stank for the rest of the game, but it's the only way they'd let me back out there."

After the game, McCarty stood at his dressing-room stall, chuckling when a misinformed reporter asked whether he had really taken 100 stitches, as had been rumored.

"Aw," he said, "the legend grows. I think it was a thousand."

Everyone laughed. But uneasily. As McCarty spoke, his damaged skin was turning green.

Man of Mystery

There are so many stories about Scotty Bowman, the coach, illustrating his myriad quirks and accomplishments. But there are so few about Scotty Bowman, the man.

"That's the way he likes it," goaltender Chris Osgood said. "He's Scotty Bowman. Nobody's ever going to know him, at least not completely."

Even in his proudest moments, he made sure of that.

Take the night of November 24, 2000. There he was again, behind the bench, sucking on ice chips, jutting his jaw like a bulldog, tilting his head back with indifference, barking at the referees, tinkering with his lines, coaching an NHL regular-season game—for the 2,000th time.

Only five others had coached 1,000 games: Al Arbour (1,606), Dick Irvin (1,449), Billy Reay (1,102), Mike Keenan (1,009), and Jacques Demers (1,006). Congratulations were coming in from colleagues around the hockey world.

"He's an elite coach at 67 years of age," Dallas Stars coach Ken Hitchcock said, knowing Bowman's vitals off the top of his head. "That's 20 years from where I am now. I don't see me at 67 coaching. I think I'll be driving the equipment truck or something. I don't think anybody can come close."

Still, there was no pomp and circumstance, no syrupy ceremony. During a stoppage in play 6:07 into the first period, Joe Louis Arena public address announcer Budd Lynch informed the crowd of the accomplishment.

A message flashed on the scoreboard screen. The fans rose to their feet. The players tapped sticks and gloves against the boards near the benches. A couple of coaches clapped, including Wings associate coach Dave Lewis. The arena roared.

And Scotty?

He just stood there.

When Lynch began, Bowman talked with his longtime associate, Barry Smith. Then he looked down at his feet. Then he stared straight ahead. Then he looked up at the screen. Then he chewed the right corner of his lower lip.

No smile. All business. As always.

When Lynch finished and the applause ebbed, Bowman looked at a player.

"Go," he said.

And the player did.

When Scotty Bowman became the first to coach 2,000 NHL games, he acted like it was just another night at the rink.

TOP TEN

Red Wings Top-Scoring Seasons

	Season	G	A	Pts.
1. Steve Yzerman	1988–1989	65	90	155
2. Steve Yzerman	1992–1993	58	79	137
3. Steve Yzerman	1989–1990	62	65	127
4. Marcel Dionne	1974–1975	47	74	121
5. Sergei Fedorov	1993–1994	56	64	120
6. Steve Yzerman	1990–1991	51	57	108
7. Sergei Fedorov	1995–1996	38	68	107
8. John Ogrodnick	1984–1985	55	50	105
9. Gordie Howe	1968–1969	44	59	103†
Steve Yzerman	1991–1992	45	58	103†

Sergei Fedorov gave the Red Wings a 3–2 victory over Vancouver by scoring his second goal of the game with 27.2 seconds left, zipping past a Canuck and swiping in a rebound.

Despite the game's exciting end, Bowman didn't loiter on the bench. He bolted, accepting only a pat on the back from Lewis as he headed into the tunnel.

"He'll celebrate," Smith said, "but he won't do it publicly."

Bowman received the game puck—someone wrote "2,000" in black marker on white hockey tape, then pasted the tape on the puck—and took a team picture in the privacy of a closed dressing room. When reporters approached, he hid the puck in his left jacket pocket.

"How do you feel?" he was asked.

"We've had better games, that's for sure," he said. "It's just that I wish we could have played a little bit better, but those things happen."

TRIVIA

What was the left-wing lock?

A. A type of padlock endorsed by Ted Lindsay in the fifties

B. A defensive system brought back from Europe by associate coach Barry Smith in the nineties

C. A move right wing Gordie Howe used to "lock up" opposing right wings in the fifties

D. A technical term for the trap New Jersey used to sweep the Red Wings in the 1995 Stanley Cup Finals

Answers to the trivia questions are on pages 185–186.

"Aren't you going to enjoy this even a little bit?"

"Nah. What are you going to do? We're going to New York."

The team was leaving for the airport in a few minutes for a game the next night against the Islanders. Bowman had just coached his 2,000th; his mind was already on his 2,001st.

Interviews finished, Bowman rushed out of the room, found his son Bob in the hall, and sneaked him the prized puck.

"See you later," he said.

Then he was gone.

"If you figure him out, he's out of the game," center Kris Draper said. "Scotty wants to have that edge."

In a Scout's Shoes

"Here," said Jim Nill, the Red Wings' assistant general manager, as he held out a piece of paper in February 2001. A visitor—the author of this book—had come to learn how scouting worked, so Nill decided to teach him.

"What's this?" the visitor asked.

"A lineup sheet," Nill said.

The visitor looked down. Looked up.

Nill was smiling.

"Tonight," Nill said, "we'll compare notes."

Uh-oh.

The visitor looked out at the ice.

Where more than a hundred experienced scouts saw a tournament featuring the best potential draft picks from the Czech Republic, Finland, Russia, and Sweden, the visitor saw a blur—a bunch of kids 18 and younger with unpronounceable names who all looked the same, whizzing around in their uniforms.

Gulp.

Don't think scouting is too tough? Try it. Just for a day.

A day like this:

Nill woke up in his hotel in Stockholm, where he had just finished scouting the Sweden Hockey Games. That was a men's tournament, featuring the best European club players from five countries. A few undrafted players were there, but mostly the field consisted of draft picks and older players who weren't in the NHL for good reasons.

Now it was time to look for fresh talent, to look at the well NHL teams would tap at the June draft. Nill was in the hotel lobby by 9:00 AM to meet Jan Blomgren, one of the Wings' Russia-based scouts, and the visitor, the wannabe scout. They piled in a car, and they were off.

Destination: Munkfors.

Munkfors? The visitor pulled out the three travel books he had bought at a Detroit-area bookstore. He flipped to the index of the first: no mention of Munkfors. He flipped to the index of the second: nothing. He flipped to the index of the third: bingo!

Page 78.

He turned to page 78. He found one sentence: "The rural idyll ends in Munkfors, where some of the best-quality steel in Europe is manufactured." He flipped to a map and found a little dot located due west of Stockholm, north of Gothenburg, not far from the Norwegian border.

Great. This is where some of the best-quality hockey prospects in Europe are manufactured?

He settled into the back seat and sighed.

Blomgren drove; Nill rode shotgun. Anticipating a journey of more than four hours through the countryside, Blomgren popped in a CD. George Michael. That wasn't too interesting, so Blomgren turned down the volume and started telling stories.

Not hockey stories.

War stories.

Blomgren wasn't a full-time scout. He scouted part-time, when he wasn't writing about Russia for *Svenska Dagbladet,* one of Sweden's two national morning newspapers. He covered the fighting in Chechnya.

For about a week at a time, Blomgren went to the front. He brought no phone and no computer, and he stuffed his money in his socks for fear of being robbed. He learned never to ride in a car in the afternoon: Russian helicopters returning from morning missions had to use their extra ammo, so they fired at random targets, and cars were random targets.

Blomgren's stories passed the time well. Before the travelers knew it, three hours had passed, and they had arrived. In Karlstad.

Karlstad? Before they could make it to Munkfors, they had to go to the airport and pick up Hakan Andersson, the Wings' director of European scouting, who is based in Stockholm but had been working somewhere else in Europe—maybe Germany, maybe the Czech Republic, or . . . the countries run together after a while.

So they picked him up, and he took the wheel, bumping Blomgren to the back, and they were off again.

Destination: Munkfors.

As Andersson drove, he briefed Nill on the players he'd seen. He talked about their height. He talked about their weight. He talked about their skills and their on-ice intelligence, which scouts call "hockey sense."

Then he talked about their hearts.

"Once you assess whether someone has enough talent, then what becomes important is the makeup of the person, the character, the drive, the desire, all the intangibles," Wings GM Ken Holland said before the trip.

A conversation in a car like this could be as important on draft day as anything. Holland and Nill could only do so much by themselves; going overseas when European leagues shut down four times a season for these national-team tournaments. The rest of the time, they had to trust their regional scouts to get to know players more intimately by talking with them, their coaches, and anyone else with information.

"You're dealing with kids," Holland said. "You don't know how they're going to adjust to a lot of money, how they're going to react to adversity. How are they going to react to being away from home? You don't know all those things.

"There's so much more involved than talent."

Andersson's evaluations passed the time well. Before they knew it, about 45 minutes had passed, and the scouts had arrived. In Sunne.

Sunne? Before they could make it to Munkfors, they had to find their hotel, check in, and check on Bruce Haralson, the Wings' western scout, who had flown in from Calgary, Alberta, where he had watched a North American prospects game.

So they found him, and they grabbed lunch, and they crammed themselves into the car like five high school buddies on a Friday night, and they were off again.

Destination: Munkfors.

Andersson guided the car along a winding, two-lane road, through a thick forest. The scenery was beautiful, breathtaking. Crisp, clear sky. Clean, clear snow. Not a soul in sight. Looking out the window left you in a trance, so Andersson turned to the visitor, who was riding shotgun now.

"Watch for moose," he said.

"Moose?"

"Yes," Andersson said. "There are more moose per square kilometer here than anywhere else in the world."

"Cool."

"Yes," Andersson said. "But we don't want to hit one. You hit a deer, you hit the deer's body. You hit a moose, you hit the moose's legs, and its body comes up over the hood and through the windshield."

"Oh."

TRIVIA

How many times have the Red Wings had the first pick in the draft and whom did they take?

Answers to the trivia questions are on pages 185–186.

The moose watch passed the time well. Before they knew it, about 30 more minutes had passed, and the scouts had arrived. In Munkfors.

Finally: Munkfors.

"When you look for players, you don't just run to the corner store," Nill said. "It's not like going to Kmart and the blue light special goes on and you grab a defenseman."

The arena was a big red barn. A white sign with blue letters read "Klingevi Ishall." The scouts walked through the door, picked up informational packets, expressed joy that they had received informational packets at all, and walked to the top of the wooden stands. If every sign they saw hadn't been in Swedish, they could have been at a community arena in Canada or the United States.

About the only attempt the tournament organizers made at the big time was the music. They played the same techno intro the Wings played before big faceoffs at Joe Louis Arena. They played the "Hockey Song." They played "Who Let the Dogs Out?"

The scouts stood. They didn't sit. They stood. They had to in order to see when the crowd rose to its feet: there were no video replays here.

"You've got to take notes when there's no play going on," Nill said. "The minute you write, something happens."

They watched back-to-back games. All around them were rivals, scouting for other organizations, and agents, scouting for themselves.

When you think of scouts, you might think of the baseball bird dog who shows up at a game, finds a jewel or two, and goes home happy. That's not the way it worked in Munkfors. *Every* scout rated *every* player.

Later, Nill would pull out his Wings-issued laptop and enter his thoughts into a computer program, which collected and organized *all* the scouts' thoughts on *all* the world's prominent players of draft age (18 years old before September 15).

By the NUMBERS

Five—Times a Red Wing has won the Calder Memorial Trophy as the NHL's rookie of the year:

Name	Season
Carl Voss	1932–1933
Jim McFadden	1947–1948
Terry Sawchuk	1950–1951
Glenn Hall	1955–1956
Roger Crozier	1964–1965

"If a kid's good, you want to know how good," said Nill, who made the final decisions on draft day. "If a kid's not good, you want to make sure he's not good."

NHL teams didn't draft to fill holes, as NBA and NFL teams did, because the vast majority of prospects took years to develop. Teams liked to draft a variety of players for balance, but mostly they just took the best player available when it was their turn. So with the help of the computer program, the Wings constantly updated lists of who they thought the best players were by region and league.

"Guys are ranking nonstop," Nill said.

When the final buzzer sounded, the five scouts rushed out of the arena to beat the crowd. Cramped in the car again, they talked about the players they had seen, agreeing more than arguing. And they watched for moose, of course.

"Who'd you like?" Andersson asked the visitor.

"Um, No. 23 from Russia."

"Yep," Nill said. "He'll go quick."

Here's the thing: recognizing the best players was so easy that one scout said his grandmother could do it. Recognizing the worst players was easy, too. While Russia's No. 23 looked like the next Igor Larionov, Russia's No. 3 treated the puck like a hot potato and shied away from hits. But the rest of the players, the mass in the middle, sorted themselves out slowly. They were pretty much all draft-worthy. But in which order? How do you decide between a 5'9" Finnish defenseman with skills and a 6' Russian forward with grit? How much weight do you put on intangibles?

How certain are you that a kid can make the long leap from Munkfors to Hockeytown?

"It's hard," Holland said.

But that's why it was so important to make the journey to Munkfors.

"We feel if you're going to get lucky for the most part in the draft, you're going to get lucky with Europeans, because they're not seen as much," Holland said. "They're playing in little, out-of-the-way places. You hope one or two surprise you."

The scouts returned to their hotel in Sunne after 9:00 PM. They gathered in the restaurant for a dinner of salmon pâté, elk, and ice cream. They couldn't talk anymore about the players they had seen because NHL Central Scouting had put together the dinner and there were competitors at surrounding tables who might eavesdrop. So they told stories, rubbed tired eyes, and consoled the visitor, who had made an unintelligible mess of notes on his lineup sheet.

"Don't worry. At first, I was as mesmerized as anyone," said Haralson, who had been scouting so long that he remembered Mark Messier as a 15-year-old. "It comes with experience."

The visitor thanked Haralson for the kind word. But he blushed, humbled just the same.

Just Plane Scary

The Red Wings, appropriately enough, were the first NHL team to take to the air. Because bad weather had made train travel impossible on December 21, 1938, general manager and coach Jack Adams chartered a DC-3 to fly the team from New York to Chicago.

"The players were upset," sportswriter Mark Beltaire said in Richard Bak's *Detroit Red Wings: The Illustrated History.* "They looked out and there was snow on the wings. I thought there was going to be a revolt."

Adams didn't do much to calm their fears.

"We were in the airport and Jack Adams started handing out quarters to all of the players," forward Carl Liscombe said in Bak's book. "They had life insurance policies in machines and he made each player buy four and make them all out to the Detroit Red Wings. That way if the plane went down, the team would at least get some money back on their investment."

The flight landed without incident.

Fear of flying was understandable in the 1930s. The thing is, it was understandable in the new millennium, too.

This was the itinerary the Wings had planned in January 2001: games at Dallas, San Jose, and Vancouver; then a couple of days to relax and practice near Phoenix; and finally games at Edmonton and Calgary.

If you had taken a map and a marker and connected the dots— down, over, up, down, *way* up, down, over—you would have had a nonsensical design that represented some nine thousand air miles. It would have been a crazy trip no matter what. But a little midair mishap added a wrinkle and made it not only crazy but scary.

The Wings beat Dallas. Then they beat San Jose. Then they got on their team plane, a DC-9 called Redbird II, and headed for Vancouver.

About 30 minutes into the flight, something went wrong.

"Everything was fine, and then all of a sudden the plane started rattling," defenseman Mathieu Dandenault said. "At first you think, 'Oh, it's just turbulence or something.' But everybody knew after a while it wasn't.

"It went on for about, maybe, 15 seconds, stopped, then another 15 seconds. By that time, the plane just started going sideways, up and down. Then we dropped. People were pretty nervous."

Engine trouble.

"The whole thing lasted about a minute," defenseman Larry Murphy said. "Then all of a sudden it was normal."

The plane made an emergency landing in Sacramento, California.

"I was somewhat surprised there was no loud applause or anything when we landed," TV broadcaster Ken Daniels said. "But I think everybody was a different shade of white, maybe."

Initial media reports were a little hysterical. The Associated Press reported the Wings had experienced a "major in-flight emergency," and a TV crew was on the scene in Sacramento just in case.

By the NUMBERS **Nine**—Times a Red Wing has won the Hart Memorial Trophy as the NHL's most valuable player:

Name	Season
Ebbie Goodfellow	1939–1940
Sid Abel	1948–1949
Gordie Howe	1951–1952
Gordie Howe	1952–1953
Gordie Howe	1956–1957
Gordie Howe	1957–1958
Gordie Howe	1959–1960
Gordie Howe	1962–1963
Sergei Fedorov	1993–1994

Sid Abel signs a new contract in 1949 after winning the Hart Memorial Trophy as the NHL's Most Valuable Player.

"I read one report that said our plane had lost two of our four engines," director of public relations John Hahn told the *Detroit Free Press*. "Well, we've only got two engines, so . . ."

Two trips by a fleet of airport shuttles took the team to a downtown hotel for the night. The Wings chartered another plane to Vancouver the next morning, got in around 2:00 PM, faced the Canucks at 7:00 PM—and, somehow, won.

"It was kind of a strange game day for us," forward Brendan Shanahan said. "But we knew a lot of people would be ready to make excuses for us if we didn't come out and play well. So I think the team took it as a challenge to come out and really have a big game."

The Wings chartered another plane to Phoenix. After being checked out by the Federal Aviation Administration and Boeing in Sacramento, Redbird II met the Wings in Phoenix to take them on the rest of their trip.

"I went out and bought a parachute yesterday," captain Steve Yzerman cracked. "I'm going to wear a parachute and an oxygen mask the whole flight."

An All-Time Low

For the Los Angeles Kings, it was an incredible comeback. For the Red Wings, it was an incredible collapse—one of the worst in their history.

But to everyone who saw it, from the 18,478 on hand at the Staples Center, to the 4,012 watching on scoreboard screens at Joe Louis Arena, to the countless others watching on television, Game 4 of the teams' first-round playoff series in 2001 was simply incredible.

Shocking.

The Wings had a 3–0 lead with less than six and a half minutes left in the third period. Then it was 3–1. And 3–2. Then it was gone. The Kings scored three goals in 5:14, the last two with their goalie pulled, the last with 53 seconds left.

And then Eric Belanger scored 2:36 into overtime, and the Kings had a 4–3 victory, tying the series at two games apiece and taking all the momentum.

"It's a great feeling," Belanger said.

"It's a tough loss," Wings forward Martin Lapointe said. "All the guys are disappointed, and they should be."

How did this happen? The Wings didn't blow third-period leads. That regular season, they had gone 32–0–2 when leading after two.

How in the world?

"There's no easy explanation," Wings forward Kirk Maltby said.

Let's start with Scott Thomas. Unlikely comeback, unlikely hero. Thomas only played because Steve Kelly had the flu, and he played just 54 seconds the first two periods. But sure enough, he was the one who scored the Kings' first playoff power-play goal against the Wings in 40 tries over two years.

By the NUMBERS

16—Years out of 20 the team didn't make the playoffs from 1967 to 1986. Things got so bad the Red Wings became known as the "Dead Things." The low point was 1985–1986, when the Wings went 17–57–6, earning 40 points. It was their worst total since they earned 38 in 1939–1940, when they played only 48 games.

The Wings were humming along, then Martin Lapointe went off for slashing Jozef Stumpel with 6:17 left. Moments later, Kings defenseman Mathieu Schneider took a shot from the point, and with 6:07 left, Thomas tapped in the puck.

Let's continue with the second goal. Unlikely collapse, unlucky breaks. Lapointe battled along the boards with Schneider and ended up off for interference with 3:22 left. While conceding he deserved the first penalty, Lapointe fumed about this one.

"If the score's 3–2, I don't think the referee calls that," Lapointe said. "It's refereeing the score, you know? It's 3–1, and it's an easy call to make, and he calls it. That's not the way it should be."

Moments later, from the corner to goaltender Chris Osgood's right, Stumpel sent the puck toward the slot. It went off one of defenseman Chris Chelios's skates, and with 2:27 left the puck squeaked between Osgood's right pad and the left post.

"Freak goal," Wings associate coach Barry Smith said.

There was question as to whether the puck crossed the goal line. Video replay officials allowed the goal, and Osgood fumed.

"The fans started cheering as if it had gone in, and their goal judge flicked the red light on," Osgood said. "I think there's absolutely no way it was in."

Let's finish with the finish. Bryan Smolinski tied the game as the Kings skated six-on-five, wristing in the puck after a scramble.

Overtime.

Adam Deadmarsh threw the puck out of the corner to Osgood's left, Ian Laperriere tipped the puck, and at 2:36 Belanger put it top shelf, streaking in off a line change.

The Wings went off looking dazed.

"We can't do much about it now: it's over," Osgood said. "They played good. We sat back. I think we deserved what we got."

Adam Deadmarsh finished off the Kings' stunning upset of the Red Wings with an overtime goal in Game 6 of their 2001 playoff series.

Before the third period, Kings coach Andy Murray motivated his players by reminding them of the "Miracle on Manchester," the greatest comeback in NHL playoff history. On April 10, 1982, the Kings rallied from a 5–0 deficit to beat Edmonton, 6–5, at the Forum, on Manchester.

"Let's make one of our own," Murray told them.

After the players obliged, the L.A. scribes tried to as well. Since Staples is located at Figueroa and 11th, at different points the *Los Angeles Times* called the thriller the "Frenzy on Figueroa," the "Fantastic Finish on Figueroa," and "Eleventh (Ave.) Heaven."

The Wings just called it embarrassing.

"What happened tonight," Wings defenseman Nicklas Lidstrom said, "shouldn't really happen."

But it did.

The Wings lost the series in six games.

A Hall of Fame Team

In the spring of 2001, the Winged Wheels had fallen off the bandwagon. The Red Wings had lost to Los Angeles in the playoffs, and some people were discouraged so much by the downward trend—Stanley Cups in 1997 and 1998, second-round losses in 1999 and 2000, first-round loss in 2001—they said it was time to break up the team.

"I remember thinking to myself, 'The team's not ready for that,'" forward Brendan Shanahan said. "Why would anyone in this city want that? This is a great time to be a hockey player and a hockey fan in the city of Detroit. You want that to last as long as possible. Talk to people in Edmonton, on Long Island. They miss those days, when it was a hot, hot ticket."

But by the fall of that year, the only people who wanted to break up the team lived in other NHL cities. What was a hot, hot ticket was now white-hot. It hurt your hand to hold it. No, the Wings weren't any younger. In fact, they were older. Fourteen of them were at least 30 years old. One was 40. But they insisted they were better. And weren't they?

They added Dominik Hasek, who had just won his sixth Vezina Trophy as the NHL's best goaltender. They added Luc Robitaille, who the previous season had scored five more goals than any Wing had. Then they added Brett Hull, who had scored two more goals the previous season than *Robitaille* had. Along the way, they made another addition, defenseman Fredrik Olausson, and several subtractions. The product looked pretty good on paper. Geez, just look at the lineup. It had nine potential Hall of Famers:

Hasek.

Hull.

Robitaille.

Shanahan.

Chris Chelios.

Sergei Fedorov.

Igor Larionov.

Nicklas Lidstrom.

Steve Yzerman.

And the coach? It was still Scotty Bowman, who had won more games than anyone else—more games than all but two men had *coached*. Bowman, needless to say, already was in the Hall of Fame. Had been for a decade.

"We're talking household names," general manager Ken Holland said, "and a number of them."

Yes. Nine.

"These," forward Darren McCarty said, "are icons of the sport."

When was the last time you saw so many on one marquee? The Colorado Avalanche was stacked. But nine potential Hall of Famers? Not quite. Surely the awesome Edmonton Oilers of the eighties. Then again, those players all made their names together on those teams; they didn't come together the way these Wings did. That was a completely different situation. Larionov said he hadn't seen a team so rich in reputations since the Soviet Union's Central Red Army, which had all of Russia's best talent before the Iron Curtain was raised. Then again, if we're throwing out completely different situations, that's about as completely different as you can get.

There had never been a team quite like this one. Oh, there had been better teams, greater teams by different measures. No question. Still, this was unique. These players had made 25 first or second postseason All-Star Teams, won 27 major individual postseason awards, combined for 60 All-Star Game appearances, combined for 90 hat tricks. Four of the top 10 active goal scorers and three of the top 10 active overall scorers were on this team.

TRIVIA

Who was the general manager of the 1997 Stanley Cup champions?

Answers to the trivia questions are on pages 185–186.

As Shanahan, who grew up a suffering Toronto Maple Leafs fan, said, "A lot of great hockey fans, unfortunately, live in the wrong city."

By the early 2000s, the Wings were trying to fight the inertia of professional sports. Championship teams are

IF ONLY ... the Red Wings had signed Jeremy Roenick in June 2001, they might not have had nine future Hall of Famers and the storybook 2002 Stanley Cup. After being wined and dined by Wings general manager Ken Holland, Roenick got a call from the Flyers in his suburban Detroit hotel room—and committed to Philadelphia. The dominoes fell differently, and the Wings ended up acquiring Dominik Hasek, Luc Robitaille, and Brett Hull.

supposed to decline. That's the way leagues are structured. The bad teams draft first, the good teams last. The bad teams are supposed to get better, the good teams worse. The standings are due to flip.

But the Wings stayed on top. They had won more games in the regular season (363) and playoffs (70) than any other team in eight years. No one had won more Cups over the decade. Only three teams out of 30—Colorado, New Jersey, and Pittsburgh—had won as many.

The Wings brought in Chelios, a three-time Norris winner, and Pat Verbeek, the only player to have 500 goals and 2,500 penalty minutes. They brought in Hasek, Hull, and Robitaille. They remembered the seventies and early eighties, the era of the Dead Things. For them, the standings were overdue to flip, as they had flipped on the Islanders and Oilers of the eighties, on the Penguins of the nineties. But the Wings were in no rush, to say the least. They had no interest in breaking up the team, not while guys like Fedorov, Lidstrom, Shanahan, and Yzerman still had good hockey left in them.

"You can't take things for granted, and that's the one thing we haven't done," senior vice president Jimmy Devellano said. "We're trying to buck the trend as long as possible. In a lot of towns, people accuse the owners and management of not trying to win. That's the one thing no one's been able to accuse us of. That's the one thing we've constantly tried to do."

The bottom line, in many ways, was the bottom line.

Owner Mike Ilitch said he would do "whatever's necessary" to keep the Wings in contention for the Cup.

"Once the city gets used to it, you get used to it," Ilitch said. "You've got to pay the price. . . . We've got to do anything we can. The Red Wings are so much a part of the city now, you just want to keep it that way."

And he kept his word.

The Wings' payroll was one of the highest in the league, much more than $60 million. Detroit might have been a small market in other sports, but in hockey, it was a big-market bully. The Wings could land the big-ticket free agents, could acquire players other teams could no longer afford.

What was remarkable was the sacrifices fans, ownership, and players made to make it happen.

The fans shelled out $51 to $80 for most seats at the Joe. And that was just in the regular season. In the playoffs, it was multiples of that. But basically, the Wings passed the money right along to the players. Almost all of what they brought in, they turned right around and spent. The Wings probably weren't going to profit unless they advanced deep into the playoffs.

"We need a heck of a run," Devellano said then. "It can't be a first-round ouster, that's for sure, or we struck out, and it's going to be quite a hit. We're taking a risk most people couldn't or wouldn't do."

The players made gaudy salaries by any standard, but they were willing to pay part of the price. Several didn't make as much as they could have elsewhere, and five players—Chelios, Hull, Lidstrom, Shanahan, and Yzerman—deferred some salary.

"There are a lot of owners and organizations that would take money and profit and put it right in their pocket," Shanahan said. "Here, it seems to always be reinvested, put toward continuing the love affair between the team and the city. Part of playing for a team like this is fitting into a budget."

But money wasn't everything. Otherwise, the New York Rangers would have been a powerhouse every year. To bring together a lineup of big names like that, the stars had to align.

Age usually was a negative when people talked about the Wings. But in many ways, the older a player was, the more likely it was he'd want to play in Detroit. Let's face it: downtown was desolate. The Joe was one of the worst rinks in the league, aesthetically speaking. The money being equal, if they had a choice, younger players might have wanted to sow their oats in a place like Chicago, Los Angeles, New York, or Toronto, places with gleaming skylines and skyboxes. But older players might have wanted to settle down in Detroit.

"It's just an excellent hockey city," Yzerman said.

So the Joe had cracked concrete, dingy stairwells, and few of the state-of-the-art amenities of other arenas. So what? That meant there were no distractions. That meant the fans came to watch the game.

"From a player's perspective, it's a great arena to play in," Yzerman said. "It's a simple arena. It's got a good atmosphere."

Yzerman also pointed out that the Joe had good ice, which further proved the point: older players had more practical priorities. Several Wings were married with children, and they said the Detroit suburbs

After Dominik Hasek joined the Red Wings in 2001, Detroit became even more of a draw for hockey talent. Luc Robitaille and Brett Hull signed that summer.

Seven—Times a Red Wing has won the Art Ross Trophy as the NHL's leading scorer:

Name	Season
Ted Lindsay	1949–1950
Gordie Howe	1950–1951
Gordie Howe	1951–1952
Gordie Howe	1952–1953
Gordie Howe	1953–1954
Gordie Howe	1956–1957
Gordie Howe	1962–1963

were great places to raise a family. The Detroit area had elite youth hockey programs, too. Don't underestimate that: it was an important factor for Chelios and Hasek, who had hockey-playing sons.

What drew stars to Detroit the most, however, was each other. They knew they gave each other the chance to win. And when you've been there, done that, when you're mature, that's all that matters.

"As you get older and you've played longer, you realize what's more fun and more important," Shanahan said. "It's a lot more fun driving home after a win than driving home after a loss in which you had a couple of goals."

The stars came because Detroit was Hockeytown; Detroit was Hockeytown because the stars came.

When the Wings won Cups four out of six years in the fifties, their boss, Jack Adams, scoffed at writers who compared the Wings to the New York Yankees: "We are not the Yankees of hockey; the Yankees are the Red Wings of baseball." Devellano wouldn't go that far in 2001, but he doesn't downplay the comparison. Both teams had tradition, glamour, some elite homegrown talent, and lots of the best players money could buy.

Both teams had something else: a big target on their backs.

"We're very similar to the New York Yankees, even to the point where a lot of people get ticked off at us," Devellano said. "A lot of people get jealous, just as they're all jealous of the Yankees."

One more thing: both the Wings and the Yankees faced incredible expectations.

The Wings set the bar so high that there was little room for success but lots for failure. In 2000–2001, the Wings finished with 111 points, the second most in the league and in franchise history. But because they lost in the first round, the season was a deep disappointment. There was only more pressure now. With the buzz came the burden.

"We understand that's the nature of the beast," Devellano said. "This is a franchise people are very passionate about now. We've created that. That's a good thing. . . . Those are expectations we just have to try to live up to."

Ask Yzerman about expectations, and he would say simply, "Our goal is to win." But not only did the Wings have to win, they had to win every night. If they lost, it was news. If they lost two straight, it was a concern. If they lost three straight, it was a crisis. What's wrong with the Wings? People would be talking about their age. People would be wondering about their egos. Everyone would be waiting for the next big blockbuster deal that would fix everything.

Many bad teams were playing in the NHL. Many good teams were playing boring hockey. The Wings wouldn't be allowed to be bad or boring. With all their stars, they needed highlights, sweet goals, sneaky passes, spectacular saves. They would be filling buildings all over North America. People were going to come out to see the best; they would expect to see it.

McCarty brought up a hockey truth: "No matter how much talent you have, in order to win, you've got to have a lot of things go right for you."

Yes. But even if injuries or bad breaks were too much to overcome, few were going to cut the Wings any slack. The cream rises, eh?

In the end, after all the smiles, all the superlatives, all the hype, all the money, they had to drink from the Cup.

Sure enough, they did.

An Important Escape

It was a beautiful Tuesday morning in Traverse City, Michigan, and the Red Wings had to take their training-camp physicals. Assistant general manager Jim Nill stood near one of the arena's two rinks, talking to a reporter about a prospect, when he stopped in midsentence.

"What's everybody looking at?" he said.

A bunch of people—players, trainers, reporters, others—were craning their necks to see through a window to the floor above. Nill went over and craned his neck, too. Through the window was a television. And on the television was a plane. And the plane was flying into a building.

Someone said terrorists had hijacked two commercial airliners and flown them into the World Trade Center towers.

It was September 11, 2001.

It was surreal. On the television, there was chaos and fire and smoke and death. On the ice, there was Chelios and Yzerman, skating, shooting pucks. On one side of the room upstairs, Wings were grunting on stationary bikes, completing one of their tests. On the other side, people were sitting in front of the television, contemplating the terrible pictures.

Shanahan sat on a plastic chair. Robitaille sat on a table. Behind them, another bunch of people—players, trainers, reporters, others—stood. They were American, Canadian, Russian, Czech, German. By then, the Pentagon was in flames, too.

No one spoke. But there was sound: hurried voices of TV anchors, grunts from Wings on bikes.

The first Trade Center tower collapsed, live, right there on the screen. A little later, the second collapsed.

One by one, the Wings left. They had a team meeting at their hotel. When the meeting was over, the players trickled into the lobby. Another surreal scene: televisions carted out and tuned to the news, volume way up; fans asking players for autographs; people on cell phones; people eating lunch; a long line of people—including several New Yorkers—from flights diverted to Traverse City, waiting to check in; golfers carrying clubs, laughing and joking.

"I've got some news," Fedorov said, holding up his cell phone.

"A plane crashed near Pittsburgh, too?" Chelios asked, shaking his head.

"Wow," forward Brent Gilchrist whispered.

"Crazy," Nill said.

In the afternoon, the Wings went ahead with their annual golf outing. It raised money for Vladimir Konstantinov and masseur Sergei Mnatsakanov, who had both been severely injured in a 1997 limousine accident. Fans had paid hundreds, thousands of dollars and traveled to Traverse City to play.

Outside, six or seven people were on a driving range, hitting little white balls onto great green grass. To the left of them, a woman was sitting still in her car. Her radio was tuned to the news. She was weeping.

At 8:45 AM the next day, exactly 24 hours after the first hijacked airliner flew into the World Trade Center, the little arena was full of fans, waiting for the Wings' first practice to begin.

At about 9:03 AM, 24 hours after the second hijacked airliner flew into the World Trade Center, Hasek appeared on the ice for the first time as a Wing, and the fans cheered.

At 9:40 AM, exactly 24 hours after the third hijacked airliner flew into the Pentagon, 39-year-old Mike Krzeminski of Traverse City stood in a corner of the arena wearing a No. 19 Yzerman sweater, trying to explain why.

"It's escapism, definitely," said Krzeminski. "You can only watch the footage so much."

While much of the sports world went silent, the Wings decided not to cancel their workouts.

"It's a delicate issue," Holland said. "Where's the line? How long do you grieve? I don't know what's right. . . . We're here, but I don't know how

By the NUMBERS

34—Players who have been captain of the Red Wings:

Name	Years
Art Duncan	1926–1927
Reg Noble	1927–1928 to 1929–1930
George Hay	1930–1931
Carson Cooper	1931–1932
Larry Aurie	1932–1933
Herbie Lewis	1933–1934
Ebbie Goodfellow	1934–1935, 1938–1939 to 1941, 1941–1942
Doug Young	1935–1936 to 1937–1938
Syd Howe	1941–1942
Sid Abel	1942–1943, 1945–1946, 1946–1947 to 1951–1952
Mud Bruneteau	1943–1944
Bill "Flash" Hollett	1943–1944, 1944–1945, 1945–1946
Ted Lindsay	1952–1953 to 1955–1956
Red Kelly	1956–1957 to 1957–1958
Gordie Howe	1958–1959 to 1961–1962
Alex Delvecchio	1962–1963 to 1972–1973, 1973–1974
Nick Libett	1973–1974, 1978–1979
Red Berenson	1973–1974
Gary Bergman	1973–1974
Ted Harris	1973–1974
Mickey Redmond	1973–1974
Larry Johnston	1973–1974
Marcel Dionne	1974–1975
Danny Grant	1975–1976, 1976–1977
Terry Harper	1975–1976
Dennis Polonich	1976–1977

Dan Maloney	1977–1978
Dennis Hextall	1977–1978, 1978–1979
Paul Woods	1978–1979
Dale McCourt	1979–1980
Errol Thompson	1980–1981
Reed Larson	1980–1981, 1981–1982
Danny Gare	1982–1983 to 1985–1986
Steve Yzerman	1986–1987 to 2003–2004, 2005–2006

much everybody's into what we're doing right now. Our hearts and minds are elsewhere."

The Wings were touched by the tragedy, in little ways, in large ways. Chelios's son was on a school trip to Arizona and couldn't get home. Several members of the organization knew Garnet "Ace" Bailey, the former Wing and the Kings' director of amateur scouting, who was among the passengers on the second plane. Bailey was on his way from Boston to Los Angeles for Kings training camp.

The Wings talked about what had happened. On the bus. In the dressing room. On the bench. Everywhere. Newspapers with screaming headlines littered the arena. As he sharpened skates, equipment manager Paul Boyer looked down at a copy of the Traverse City *Record-Eagle* sitting on the table. The headline: Terror Hits Home.

"How crazy is that?" Boyer said.

Was it crazy to play hockey? Maybe. Maybe not.

"You know, I think everybody wanted to skate, to try to forget a little about it," defenseman Steve Duchesne said. "I don't know what to say, if we should have, if we shouldn't have."

Was it crazy for hundreds of fans to show up? Maybe. Maybe not.

Jill and Fred Banister, both 58, of Traverse City, stood behind one of the goals.

"Just last week," Fred said, "we were on top of the World Trade Center."

Pause.

"It was such a magnificent sight."

Pause.

"I just can't imagine the horror those people must have felt."

The Banisters had felt enough horror of their own. Their daughter and her fiancé lived in New York. Their son and daughter-in-law lived in Washington, D.C. They had spent hour after hour after hour September 11 trying to get through to their loved ones, just trying to see if they were alive. Their daughter's fiancé worked near the World Trade Center. An eternity. That's what it took for them to find out everything was all right.

Fred shook his head.

"We saw so much tragedy yesterday . . ."

Hockey was all they wanted to see today.

They had promised their son long ago they would take an Yzerman poster to training camp and get it autographed. Hundreds of miles away from the rubble, helpless but to hope and pray and maybe give a little blood, they weren't going to break their promise. Some say an autograph is a meaningless thing, but is it?

"I can't do anything [to help], but this is something I can do," Jill said. "That might sound silly, but . . ."

She held her head in her hands.

If the Wings didn't know their role in society—as entertainers, as examples—they knew it now. They approached the team's public relations staff and suggested they give blood.

"It just sounded like a good idea," Yzerman said. "We said, 'We should probably do that.'"

The Northwest Michigan Blood Program sent a mobile blood bank to the arena, and about 20 members of the organization gave. Sharon Childs, the program's director of donor services, limited the Wings to 20 pints. The blood itself wasn't as important as what it meant.

"You know," Childs said, "we need national symbols to say, 'Come on, America, stand up and do what you can.'"

Long-Distance Connection

The night Luc Robitaille scored his first goal for the Red Wings, October 12, 2001, he was in tears. He had to say good-bye.

It was after a victory over the Buffalo Sabres at Joe Louis Arena.

He was off to New York for a game against the Islanders. His wife, Stacia, and their sons, 13-year-old Steven and 6-year-old Jesse, were off to Los Angeles. Stacia had work, and the boys had school.

Luc looked at the little guy, Jesse. But the little guy wouldn't look back. He couldn't look back. They weren't going to see each other for a month.

"He was crying, and Luc started to cry, and I thought, 'This is so hard,'" Stacia said. "It broke our hearts."

This was another side of NHL life, a side rarely seen by the public. Luc lived in an apartment in suburban Detroit, and Stacia and the boys lived in the family home near Los Angeles, some two thousand miles away.

Luc and Stacia sat down and had a long talk after the 2000–2001 season. Luc had played 15 years in the NHL, 12 of them in Los Angeles. They loved it there. But the Kings had offered a one-year, $2.5 million contract—a $1 million pay cut. What's more, to the Robitailles, the Kings weren't making a commitment to win, and Luc was longing for a Stanley Cup. He had never won one.

Stacia told Luc the time had come for him to go—and go to a winner.

"I agreed with her," Luc said.

So they talked about what that would mean.

Three times in his career, Luc had been traded: Los Angeles to Pittsburgh, Pittsburgh to the Rangers, New York back to Los Angeles. Each time, the family moved as a unit. But this time, it wouldn't.

By the NUMBERS

Four—Times a Red Wings coach has won the Jack Adams Award as the NHL's coach of the year:

Name	Season
Bobby Kromm	1977–1978
Jacques Demers	1986–1987
Jacques Demers	1987–1988
Scotty Bowman	1995–1996

Stacia had a career, too. She was a recording artist with an album, *Hush,* coming out. She was president of her own label, Raystone Records.

And Steven's school was a big factor.

And . . . well, they had to do what they had to do.

"We made the decision together, my wife and I," Luc said. "We talked about it, how we had to communicate, how we would take trips to see each other, how we had to stick together the whole year. We knew it would be hard."

When the Wings offered a contract that July, they guaranteed two years, $9 million, and a shot at Stanley. Luc signed.

And he left L.A.

The phone became the family's best friend.

"We talk every day—two, three times a day," Luc said.

"Some days, it's 20 times a day," Stacia said. "We just call each other constantly back and forth."

"I think that's really what's keeping us together," Luc said.

The boys had Dad on speed dial. Every now and then, the little guy, Jesse, would hit the button at home in L.A., Luc would pick up in Detroit, and Jesse would say something like, "Dad, I'm looking for my hockey stick. Do you know where it is?"

Some nights, Luc and Stacia would watch television together— almost a continent apart—by sitting on their respective couches with their respective phones.

But even more important than the phone calls were the plane rides to see each other.

One reunion was really, really special.

Luc Robitaille scored most of his goals as a Los Angeles King. But he scored number 600 in Anaheim as a Red Wing.

After that heartbreaking scene with Luc and the little guy in tears saying good-bye, Stacia got an idea. In a week, Luc would face the Kings in Detroit for the first time since signing with the Wings. The game was on a Saturday. She didn't have work. The kids didn't have school.

"How great would that be to turn around and go back?" she thought.

So they came back for the weekend—as a surprise.

They took a flight out the day of the game. On the plane, Stacia's cell phone rang. It was Luc. She answered, pretending she was in L.A. Then without warning, she hung up on him. The flight attendant was speaking over the intercom, and Stacia didn't want to give herself away.

Luc called back. Stacia answered again, pretended again, hung up on him again. This happened three or four times. Finally, as Stacia and the boys were driving down to the Joe, Luc asked what the heck was going on.

"Hon, I'm sorry," Stacia told him. "I have such a bad connection here."

He had no idea.

The horn sounded, and the teams went off for the first intermission tied, 2–2.

"Hey," someone said to Luc, "your kids are here."

"I was like, 'What?'" Luc said. "It didn't even make sense."

The guards let Steven and Jesse come down into the hallway outside the dressing room, so when Luc came out for the second period, they were waiting for him, his biggest fans, yelling, "LUUUC!"

"What a shock," Luc said.

"He just had instant tears," Stacia said.

That period, Luc went out and scored, and the Wings beat L.A.

Chris and Kris

Hockey is full of comings and goings and reunions, and all the emotions and strange situations that go with them.

On November 2, 2001, goaltender Chris Osgood came back to Detroit. Beforehand, he just wanted to get it over with. Play well. Win one for the New York Islanders. Move on. He had spent eight seasons with the Red Wings, only to be let go via the waiver draft because of Dominik Hasek's arrival. He was glad he didn't have to come back to Joe Louis Arena again that season. But by that morning, he felt differently.

"Now," he said, "I'm thinking it would be nice to come back some more."

For a while, it seemed Osgood never had left. The night before, he called Kris Draper, his good friend, and he spent time at his Detroit-area home with his wife and child, who weren't going to join him on Long Island until later in the month. That morning, he rode down to the rink with Manny Legace, another good friend, and he spent time in the Wings' training room with more good friends.

"We just talked about the kind of stuff you talk about with a buddy who has a new job at a new office down the hall," forward McCarty said, shrugging.

Eventually, Osgood made his way to that new office, the visitors' dressing room.

"I'm sure it's the first time he's ever seen that area," Draper said.

Although his uniform was blue and orange, Osgood put on the same red goalie pads he wore with the Wings, because he hadn't broken in his new ones yet. As the Islanders stretched for practice, the Red Wings trainer John Wharton ribbed him from the Detroit bench.

"Cut the cord!" he yelled, smiling. "If you let us go, we'll let you go!"

Then Wharton turned back into the tunnel.

Quietly, he said, "Nah, we'll never let him go. He's the best."

Osgood realized he had to let go. He felt a surge of pride looking up at the Wings' Cup banners, knowing he played a large role in winning two of them. But he put that out of his mind. This was not the time.

"When I retire and come back to Detroit, then I can reminisce about what I did in Detroit," Osgood said. "But right now, I think it would be unfair to my teammates and the coaches and people in New York if I continuously talk about what I did in Detroit and winning Cups, because now I want to win a Cup in New York."

Chris Osgood has gotten a lot of grief at times in Detroit. But he trails only Terry Sawchuk in Red Wings victories.

He smiled.

"I had a great time in Detroit, and now I'm having a great time in New York," he said. "So I'm pretty spoiled."

Draper's wife, Julie, and Osgood's wife, Jenna, watched the game together. They sat in section 121, lower bowl, right on the red line. They shared popcorn. Their husbands had lived together before they were married and were roommates on the road.

The wives laughed about the first game between the buddies, earlier in the season on Long Island, when Draper broke in on Osgood—and passed.

"He was taking it easy on him," Julie said.

The play led to the winning goal, but in their many phone conversations, Osgood ribbed Draper.

"Oh, I heard about it," Draper said, smiling.

Draper wanted another chance at bragging rights. Asked about all the hoopla surrounding Osgood's return, he said, "Let's get it out of the way—then fill the net on him."

The Islanders scored on their first shot. But what do you know? Later in the first period, Draper stole the puck in the neutral zone, raced down the right wing, and snapped a

TRIVIA

Which Red Wings great is the only player to have led the NHL in scoring and penalty minutes?

A. Gordie Howe

B. Ted Lindsay

C. Bob Probert

D. Dino Ciccarelli

Answers to the trivia questions are on pages 185–186.

shot. Osgood got a piece of the puck with his blocker, but not enough. It dropped across the goal line, and the game was tied.

"Before the game, because he had faced him so much in practice, he was thinking about a new strategy," Julie said. "He must have found a new hole that Ozzie didn't know he knew about."

The fans used to chant, "OZ-ZIE! OZ-ZIE!"

Now they taunted, "OS-GOOOD! OS-GOOOD!"

And now, what do you know? In the second period, deep in the corner to Osgood's right, defenseman Maxim Kuznetsov threw the puck in front. Only once in more than three seasons had Draper scored two goals in a game, but here he held off Michael Peca, held his stick with one hand, and tipped the puck past his buddy. Draper celebrated what

TOP TEN

Red Wings Shutouts

	Name	Shutouts
1.	Terry Sawchuk	85
2.	Chris Osgood	32
3.	Harry Lumley	26
4.	Roger Crozier	20
5.	Clarence Dolson	17†
	Glenn Hall	17†
	Harry Holmes	17†
	Norm Smith	17†
9.	Roy Edwards	14
10.	John Mowers	13†
	Manny Legace	13†

turned out to be the winning goal with a big smile, throwing his arms into the air.

"OS-GOOOD! OS-GOOOD!"

"After the first goal, Kris was laughing the whole time; my Chris was mad," Jenna said. "After the second goal, my Chris was really mad."

The wives laughed.

"I told him I'd never talk to him again if he scored on my husband," Jenna said. "It's going to be a long time now."

The wives laughed again.

"After the game," Julie said, "they'll be laughing about this."

Oh, they were.

Draper, in the Detroit dressing room: "It was two good friends just going out and having fun, playing a fun hockey game. We'll laugh about it. For sure we will."

Osgood, in the New York dressing room: "I'll get a good laugh with Drapes someday. But I'll get him back. You put that in the paper: I'll get him back one day. . . . He was laughing a couple of times. But I was laughing, too, when he fumbled a breakaway [in the third period]."

Draper, back in the Detroit dressing room: "I definitely would love to have that one back. Lucky for him, or we would be talking about three goals, not two."

Osgood, back in the New York dressing room: "Our wives are sitting together. They took the kids out to Halloween the other night. Then he does that to me."

Back and forth they went.

"It's all in fun," Osgood said. "We were laughing about it on the ice."

Pause.

"It's kind of ironic," he said, "isn't it?"

A Long Drive

Brendan Shanahan's personality made him not only one of the most popular Red Wings but also one of the most popular players, period. He's smart, witty, funny. But he also has an Irish temper—and one time it sparked a chain of events that ended with him sitting in a car on the side of a rainy Canadian highway getting an earful from a high-ranking NHL official.

The Wings suffered an overtime loss at Los Angeles on November 10, 2001. After they left the Staples Center for a red-eye flight back to Detroit, the final game summary still wasn't available. A reporter asked an L.A. media relations official why, and the official said two penalties needed to be added: a minor for throwing an object onto the ice and a 10-minute misconduct, both to Shanahan.

"What happened?"

"He threw a water bottle at the referees."

The incident had been missed by almost everyone in the postgame commotion.

The Wings were off the next day. Without being able to talk to Shanahan, who later said he threw the bottle aimlessly, the reporter noted in the final paragraph of a story inside the *Free Press* sports section that Shanahan had thrown the bottle "at" the referees.

Uh-oh.

A Toronto TV station read the story and blew it up the next day, and so it came to the attention of Colin Campbell, the NHL's vice president of hockey operations—or Mr. Discipline.

Campbell was not pleased.

Early in the season, Shanahan had ripped the referees.

Brendan Shanahan is known for his skill and sense of humor, but he is also known for his Irish temper. He has battled with the officials at times.

"It's ridiculous," he had said. "In the three games I've seen so far this year, it's just a joke what's happening to this league. I'm all for protecting players and eliminating dirty plays from the NHL, but you know, divers are being rewarded in this league, and without addressing it, the league is losing some of its integrity."

One night, Shanahan received a gross misconduct after a game. Why?

"I guess I was gross," Shanahan said.

The Wings took four minors in the third period, and Shanahan took the last for slashing with one minute left. Earlier, an errant stick had cut Shanahan's left cheek, but the referees hadn't called anything.

"They refused to believe I was cut with a stick," Shanahan said.

By the NUMBERS

11—Times a Red Wing has won the Lady Byng Memorial Trophy for sportsmanship, gentlemanly conduct, and a high standard of playing ability:

Name	Season
Marty Barry	1936–1937
Bill Quackenbush	1948–1949
Red Kelly	1950–1951
Red Kelly	1952–1953
Red Kelly	1953–1954
Dutch Reibel	1955–1956
Alex Delvecchio	1958–1959
Alex Delvecchio	1965–1966
Alex Delvecchio	1968–1969
Marcel Dionne	1974–1975
Pavel Datsyuk	2005–2006

After the final horn, Shanahan flipped referee Shane Heyer the puck, as if giving him the game puck for a good effort. Then he clapped his gloves and smiled. Obviously, he was being sarcastic.

"It was a good game," Shanahan said. "I just thought, with two first-place teams playing tonight, we should be able to play five-on-five in the third period. I said some things in the end maybe I shouldn't have. But the game was over at that point. I voiced some frustration."

Shanahan was fined $1,000, the maximum allowed under the collective bargaining agreement.

Campbell asked the Kings to send him a tape of the water-bottle toss. Someone, whom he identified only as a member of the Wings organization, told him Shanahan had knocked the bottle off the bench with his stick. But the tape showed that the bottle, as Campbell put it, "was whistled across, spiraled . . . like Brett Favre threw it." The bottle had cleared the Kings streaming off the bench and had slid on the ice in the direction of the referees.

What's more, league officials felt Shanahan had been complaining about diving—yet was diving himself.

"That's what really pissed us off," Campbell said.

A fine wouldn't do.

"It's easy to fine a guy $1,000; it's easy for a guy to get fined $1,000," Campbell said. "It has no impact."

So Campbell came up with something novel.

"I said," Campbell recalled, "'Look, we've had something before, you've made some comments in the paper this year, and that's enough. You've always got an excuse. Come and talk to me. We'll talk about it.'"

On an awful afternoon—rainy, foggy, misty—Shanahan had to cross the border from the United States to Canada, drive about two and a half hours on the 401, and stop at a little parking spot when he reached the Highway 19 interchange, between Woodstock, New York, and London, Ontario. He had to meet Campbell, who was based in Toronto, lived in a small Ontario town, and was on his way to one of his son's hockey games.

"He got out of his car and came into my car," Campbell said. "We sat there and talked for a half hour. . . . He had some issues with the refereeing. I said, 'This is how it is: at the end of the day, calls are made. They might be right, and they might be wrong. You have bad games. Well, the referees have bad games. But you can't take it into your own hands. The league's good. The league's good to you.'"

Shanahan drove back to Detroit in the dark. The league didn't have a problem with him the rest of the season.

Fire and Ice

Igor Larionov was a lot of things when he played for the Red Wings from 1995 to 2003 (except for a stint with the Florida Panthers in 2000). The man they called the "Professor" was a Russian legend, a deft passer, a mentor, a lover of soccer and politics, a wine connoisseur.

Not to mention a hero.

"He literally saved our lives and our house," Bob Ray said.

Larionov arrived home late the night of January 20, 2002, after setting up an overtime goal in a 3–2 victory over the Ottawa Senators. He had no idea he was about to make another, far more important assist.

As he tried to unwind with his wife, Elena, they smelled something strange.

Smoke.

The house next door was on fire.

Larionov ran outside, ran to the neighbors' front door, screamed, banged, rang the bell, and woke up Ray and his wife, Suzanne. They had no idea what was going on. They had been sound asleep with their cats, Wild Thing, Alley Cat, and Snickers. Their bedroom was way back in their ranch home, and the fire had ignited in the garage, where Bob had disposed of fireplace ashes he hadn't realized were still hot.

"Mr. Ray and his wife are very lucky people," said Tim Wangler, Birmingham assistant chief fire marshal.

The Larionovs called 911 at 12:31 AM. The flashing lights came, and the fire was out in 20 to 30 minutes. Just in time. It had started to spread from the garage to the attic, where it could have spread quickly through the whole house.

"If it had been 15 minutes later we wouldn't have had a house," Ray said. "We're very fortunate."

Left outside in his underwear, with no shoes and in the snow, Ray had nowhere to go. He and Suzanne couldn't return to their house. So the Larionovs brought the Rays into their house. Clothed them. Served them tea. Kept them company until almost dawn, when they left to stay with a relative.

"They were very hospitable," said Wangler, who interviewed the Rays at the Larionovs'. "It's the way it should be: neighbors helping neighbors."

Larionov declined to comment on the incident. Wings spokesman John Hahn said Larionov played down his actions, saying, "Anybody

Igor Larionov does it all: he shoots, he scores, and after the game, he saves his neighbors when their house catches fire.

By the NUMBERS

26—Men who have been head coach of the Red Wings:

Coach	Years	Record
Art Duncan	1926–1927	10–21–2
Duke Keats	1926–1927	2–7–2
Jack Adams	1927–1928 to 1946–1947	13–390–161
Tommy Ivan	1947–1948 to 1953–1954	262–118–90
Jimmy Skinner	1954–1955 to 1957–1958	123–78–46
Sid Abel	1957–1958 to 1967–1968, 1969–1970	340–339–132
Bill Gadsby	1968–1969 to 1969–1970	35–31–12
Ned Harkness	1970–1971	12–22–4
Doug Barkley	1970–1971, 1975–1976	20–46–11
Johnny Wilson	1971–1972 to 1972–1973	67–56–22
Ted Garvin	1973–1974	2–9–1
Alex Delvecchio	1973–1974 to 1974–1975, 1975–1976	53–81–21
Billy Dea*	1975–1976 to 1976–1977, 1981–1982	32–57–11
Larry Wilson	1976–1977	3–29–4
Bobby Kromm	1977–1978 to 1979–1980	79–111–41
Marcel Pronovost**	1979–1980	2–7–0
Ted Lindsay	1980–1981	3–14–3
Wayne Maxner	1980–1981 to 1981–1982	34–68–27
Nick Polano	1982–1983 to 1984–1985	79–127–34
Harry Neale	1985–1986	8–23–4
Brad Park	1985–1986	9–34–2
Jacques Demers	1986–1987 to 1989–1990	137–136–47

Bryan Murray	1990–1991 to 1992–1993	124–91–29
Scotty Bowman***	1993–1994 to 2001–2002	410–203–88
Dave Lewis	2002–2003 to 2003–2004	96–47–21
Mike Babcock	2005–2006	58–24

*Delvecchio was officially head coach late in 1975–1976 and early in 1976–1977, but Dea worked behind the bench. Dea took over for Maxner late in 1981–1982.

**Lindsay was officially head coach the last nine games of 1979–1980, but Pronovost worked behind the bench.

***Lewis and fellow associate coach Barry Smith worked behind the bench the first five games of 1998–1999 while Bowman was out for medical reasons. They went 4–1–0.

would've done it," and he was just glad he was in the right place at the right time.

Nevertheless, Wangler said, "He was instrumental in saving their lives, getting them out. It was one of those happy outcomes. You hate to see the fire. It was devastating to the Rays. But it could have been so much worse."

The day the news broke, thanks to teasing teammates, in his locker Larionov found a red-plastic toy fireman's helmet.

Fight Club

In the late 1990s and early 2000s, it was simple: if a Detroit goaltender fought Colorado goaltender Patrick Roy, the Red Wings won the Stanley Cup.

Mike Vernon fought Roy in 1996–1997, and the Wings won the Cup. Chris Osgood fought Roy in 1997–1998, and the Wings won the Cup. Dominik Hasek fought Roy in 2001–2002 . . . well, at least he *tried* to.

It was a late regular-season game in Denver, and Roy was going after Wings forward Kirk Maltby, because he thought Maltby had run into him intentionally.

"He was getting eye-gouges in there," Maltby said. "It was like a wrestling match."

All hell broke loose. With six Avs on five Wings, Hasek left his crease and bolted down the ice, fiddling with his glove and blocker to get them off as he went.

As the Wings and their fans watched, their minds flashed back to the past and forward to the future.

Sure, they knew the history of Vernon and Osgood. But Hasek was brought in to beat Roy, not beat him up. These were two of the game's greatest goaltenders—Hasek with two Hart Memorial Trophies as most valuable player and six Vezina Trophies as top goaltender, Roy with three Conn Smythe Trophies as playoff MVP and three Vezinas—not two of the game's greatest gladiators. The playoffs were three and a half weeks away, and if Hasek got hurt . . .

As Hasek closed in, he slipped on Roy's discarded stick and tumbled. The brawl became a blooper. Hasek got up, but before he and Roy could throw down, the officials separated them.

IF ONLY . . . the Red Wings hadn't embarrassed Patrick Roy so badly December 2, 1995, he might not have become such a pain to them later. In their final visit to the Montreal Forum, the Wings routed the Canadiens, 11–1. Roy wasn't pulled until he had allowed nine goals, and he was so upset that he told the team president he had played his last game for the Habs. He was quickly traded to Colorado.

"I was pretty upset at the moment," Hasek said. "The referee grabbed me. I wanted to be involved. It's part of the game."

"He was probably trying to prove something. I don't know what it was," Roy told *The Denver Post*. "I think it would have been more interesting if the ref had not been there."

Patrick Roy and Dominik Hasek are civil here, but Hasek went after Roy one day in 2002, as Red Wings goalies had done before.

By the NUMBERS

Five—Numbers retired by the Red Wings:

Name	Number
Terry Sawchuk	1
Ted Lindsay	7
Gordie Howe	9
Alex Delvecchio	10
Sid Abel	12

"I respect Patrick Roy," Hasek said. "However, if something like that happens, I am ready anytime. I know there is a tradition in Detroit that every time a goalie is involved in a fight with Patrick Roy, Detroit wins the Stanley Cup."

Wings forward Brendan Shanahan thanked God that Hasek hadn't fought Roy. Wings forward Brett Hull said what Hasek and Roy had done was "idiotic." Wings coach Scotty Bowman said Hasek had scored points with his teammates and the most important thing was that he hadn't gotten hurt. As it turned out, Hasek ended up with a back injury.

But Hasek sat out only one game, and of course, the Wings won the Cup. The near miss must have been good enough for the hockey gods.

The next season, after Hasek retired, people asked Wings goaltender Curtis Joseph if he would carry on the tradition.

"You know what? I don't premeditate those things," Joseph said. "My ideal objective would be to get in there and get two points and go home."

Joseph didn't fight Roy. The Wings were swept in the first round of the playoffs by Anaheim.

The Captain

Steve Yzerman's leadership was legendary. That's why he was known in and around Detroit simply as "the Captain." And nothing illustrated his ability better than the Red Wings' first-round playoff series with Vancouver in 2002.

What he did on the ice was impressive enough. After sitting out 27 of the previous 30 regular-season games because of a bad right knee that would need radical surgery, he endured all sorts of hardship—from pain-killing injections to using his stick as a crutch to get up when he fell—and returned to face the Canucks. At age 37, he made big plays, made them at big times, and led the Wings in scoring in the series with three goals and five assists.

What he did off the ice, however, was even more impressive.

The Wings had a roster that featured nine potential Hall of Famers and was by far the best team in the regular season. But they had coasted down the stretch and were facing the hottest team in the league, and they fell behind in the series, 2–0.

There was panic in Detroit at the end of Game 2. The fans had been shouting to the scorers, "Shoot the puck!" They had been riding goaltender Dominik Hasek.

Yzerman quickly stripped off his gear, showered, dressed in his street clothes, and made himself available for interviews, drawing reporters to himself and away from his teammates.

He was calm.

"I don't think we've been outplayed in either of the two games we've lost, but we're just not quite there," he said. "Our power play isn't there. Maybe we're not as sharp as we should be, not as cohesive as we should be. I don't know if that's because of the stretch run or not."

They call him "Stevie." They call him "Stevie Y." But mostly, out of respect for his leadership, people in Detroit call Steve Yzerman "the Captain."

IF ONLY . . . Dan Cloutier had stopped Nicklas Lidstrom's red-line shot, the Red Wings might have lost in the first round instead of winning the Stanley Cup in 2002. Vancouver had a 2–0 series lead, and Game 3 was tied at 1 in the final moments of the second period, when Lidstrom fired a 90-footer that somehow eluded Cloutier. The Wings won the game—and the next three, too.

He was diplomatic.

"People here, they want the team to win; they want the team to do well," he said. "I've been through it before. There's high expectations. So I'm not really concerned about it. The thing is, we know when to shoot the puck. You want to shoot the puck, but you can't shoot it into three people."

He was defiant.

"Before the series is over, you're going to say, 'That Dom, he's an unbelievable goalie. He played fantastic for Detroit,'" he said. "I'm not concerned about goaltending at all. He's a fantastic goalie and will prove it."

Asked if he still expected the series to go the distance, he lowered his eyebrows.

"Maybe not," he said, firmly.

Pause.

"Doesn't mean we're going to lose, either."

The Wings flew to Vancouver that night. Before practice the next afternoon, Yzerman stood up in the dressing room and spoke for three or four minutes as if reading from a cue card.

"We just had a brief little meeting," Yzerman said.

Asked what he told the team, Yzerman said, "I thought despite losing the first two we did a lot of good things. The thing we couldn't do was beat ourselves up. So again it was, 'Let's just relax. We'll be ready for the game. Go out and play hockey.' . . .

"At some point in the playoffs—unfortunately it was after two games— you're faced with a must-win game. It's how you respond in that one. Either you respond and play well, or you go home. Been through it before. So we're comfortable that, 'Hey, if we just win, we're all right. We're in good shape. It's not the end of the world.' Coming in here down, 2–zip, we felt pretty good about ourselves and our chances of winning this series."

By the NUMBERS **19**—Consecutive seasons Steve Yzerman was the Red Wings' captain. That's the NHL record for wearing the C on the sweater. He became the youngest captain in team history at age 21 in 1986–1987, and he was captain until he retired at age 41 in July 2006.

Yzerman said his speech "wasn't anything brilliant."

Teammate Kris Draper agreed, saying, "He just said the things we all knew. I mean, that's it. Game 1, we had that slip away. We realized that. We knew we just had to be better and get better."

But, Draper added, "He's the kind of guy, when he steps up the whole room just listens. He picks his spots. That's why he's such a great leader. A guy can say things, but he goes out and backs everything up."

The series didn't go the distance. The Wings didn't lose, either. They won four straight and won it in six.

A Master's Touch

No one but Scotty Bowman—with his touch, experience, and presence—could have handled a situation like this.

The Red Wings and their archrival, the Colorado Avalanche, went to Game 7 in the 2002 Western Conference finals. The Wings were under tremendous pressure to win the Stanley Cup, having acquired Dominik Hasek, Luc Robitaille, and Brett Hull in the off-season, giving the team nine potential Hall of Famers. A loss would have been devastating.

Although the Wings were coming off a victory and playing at home, things didn't look good. Hasek was 0–2 in Game 7s; Roy was 6–5. The Wings hadn't played a Game 7 since 1996 and hadn't played one this important since the 1964 finals, which they lost to the Toronto Maple Leafs; the Avs had won six consecutive elimination games—including their past four Game 7s. Roy had a 0.50 goals-against average and a .980 save percentage in those six games.

"He's been proven the best in this situation over the years," Colorado captain Joe Sakic said.

The Detroit area was on edge. The fans showed up early, some standing outside holding homemade signs, to greet the players as they arrived at Joe Louis Arena. Captain Steve Yzerman strolled in as if this were Nashville on a Monday night in November, coffee cup in his left hand, black leather coat slung over his right shoulder. But few others were so calm.

As the Wings dressed for warm-ups, Bowman walked around the center of the room. He had barked at them when they led the series, 2–1. He had backed off when they trailed the series, 3–2. Now, he told them stories. This was his ninth Game 7, tying him for the NHL record with one of his protégés, Mike Keenan. Here were all those great

TOP TEN

Red Wings Playoff Shutouts

Name	Shutouts
1. Terry Sawchuk	11
2. Chris Osgood	9
3. Dominik Hasek	6t
Harry Lumley	6t
5. Glen Hanlon	3t
Norm Smith	3t
7. John Mowers	2t
Earl Robertson	2t
Mike Vernon	2t
10. Roger Crozier	1t
Wilf Cude	1t
Bill Ranford	1t
John Ross Roach	1t
Greg Stefan	1t
Cecil Thompson	1t

players, listening like little kids, listening as they would to perhaps no other coach.

What other coach could talk about the old days when lower-level teams played best-of-*nine* series instead of best-of-seven series, because they needed the money? What other coach could recall a series that went *10* games, because overtime went so long in the ninth game that the game was stopped and replayed? Bowman told the team about a player who scored a crucial goal in that series.

He turned to Kris Draper. He had promoted Draper from checking line center to right wing with playmaking center Sergei Fedorov and sharp-shooting left wing Brendan Shanahan much of the season, and Draper had responded by posting career highs in goals (15), points (30), and plus-minus (plus-26). Still, Draper had little scoring touch: it seemed he couldn't score on a breakaway to save his life. Bowman said that player from the old days had stone hands.

"Kind of like you, Drapes."

The Wings broke up in laughter.

Bowman told them the game would be memorable no matter what happened, to just go out and play.

"He doesn't come in and give big speeches," Shanahan said. "But certainly in big games and big moments, when you've got a guy that's been coaching as long as he has and can draw off his successes and experience, it can exude confidence to the players. I think he's one of those guys that if he believes it'll happen, that can rub off."

The Wings went out and heaped an avalanche on the Avalanche, scoring on their first shot, their second shot, their third shot, and so on, winning the most lopsided Game 7 in NHL history, 7–0. Roy, the best in this situation over the years, lasted little more than two periods.

"You imagine and pray for something like this, but you don't realistically think it's going to happen," Hull said. "A couple of us talked on the bench. We just said, 'We keep looking up at the clock in disbelief at the score.'"

Bowman. Then belief. Then disbelief.

Funny how Scotty tells a story, and in the end, it tells a story about him.

IF ONLY . . . Patrick Roy hadn't dropped the puck, the Red Wings might have lost to the archrival Avalanche in the Western Conference finals instead of winning the Stanley Cup in 2002. In Game 6, Roy made a spectacular save on Steve Yzerman—and a spectacular mistake. He stood up and raised his glove to show off. The puck fell into the crease, and Brendan Shanahan knocked it in. Colorado lost, 2–0, then lost Game 7, 7–0.

The Old Man and OT

Game 3 of the 2002 Stanley Cup Finals was an epic, maybe not as much of an epic as the opener of the 1936 playoffs, the game Mud Bruneteau ended in the sixth overtime, but an epic nonetheless.

The Red Wings and the Carolina Hurricanes were tied at one game apiece. With less than two minutes left in the third period, the Wings trailed, 2–1. Their karma was bad: captain Steve Yzerman had hit the left post with a shot midway through the first, and defenseman Steve Duchesne had hit a shot off the right post early in the third. But they were confident.

"You have got so many great players and so many guys that can score goals, you never feel like you are out of it," right wing Brett Hull said.

Late in the third period, the officials whistled for a faceoff in the Carolina zone. Coach Scotty Bowman didn't pull goaltender Dominik Hasek, but he put out a power-play-type unit—Hull, Yzerman, Sergei Fedorov, Nicklas Lidstrom, and Brendan Shanahan—searching for yet another late-game goal. Yzerman beat Rod Brind'Amour, a fellow faceoff expert, and drew the puck back to the right point. Fedorov sent it across the blue line. Lidstrom fired a wrist shot, and Hull, holding out his stick in the slot, tipped the puck past goaltender Arturs Irbe. The game was tied, 2–2.

One minute, 14 seconds remained.

Hull said the play was "dumb luck," but Shanahan said Hull had such awesome hand-eye coordination, that it was "not an accident he got his stick on it."

Lidstrom hit a shot off the left post with 50 seconds left. Yzerman cut in on goal with one second left.

The horn sounded: overtime.

The Wings' history was bad: they were 1–4 in OT in the playoffs, the Hurricanes 7–1. But they were confident.

They kept getting chances. At 8:35, center Pavel Datsyuk made Gretzky-esque moves, stick-handling past forward Sami Kapanen, then defenseman Marek Malik. But Irbe got his left pad on the puck. At 12:44, one-timing a pass from Fedorov on a two-on-one, Shanahan fired left of a yawning net, wide by inches.

Shanahan shook his head on the bench. This, after putting a shot off the post with an empty net in Game 5 of the Western Conference finals against the archrival Colorado Avalanche. This, when he had one goal in his past 10 games, a tap-in.

"Good thing I didn't have a knife," Shanahan said, "or I would've slit my throat."

At 15:35, defenseman Fredrik Olausson hit the crossbar.

"You start to wonder if it's ever going to go in," Olausson said.

The horn blew: second overtime.

The Hurricanes killed a penalty. The Wings killed a penalty—while Hasek fell, displaying his biggest weakness: wandering from the net.

"Sometimes I think he gets bored," forward Darren McCarty said.

"With Dom," Yzerman said, "we leave him alone and assume he knows what he's doing."

At 16:39, at the end of a pretty passing play, Shanahan sent the puck from the right wing across the slot. Yzerman put it on net, but Kapanen got his stick on it, and Irbe dived and snagged it with his glove. Yzerman rolled head over heels, then appeared to swear and say, "I don't believe it!"

Shanahan sighed.

"I was thinking," he said, "'Well, at least I'm not the only guy.'"

The horn sounded: third overtime.

In the Carolina dressing room, players were taking fluid intravenously. In the Detroit dressing room, things were relatively routine.

"When you are in a tight situation, you come in between periods, and Steve Yzerman is talking like he's about to fall asleep," Hull said. "He's so calm, but his words just ring loud."

Some guys kept most of their equipment on; some guys stripped to their underwear. Some taped sticks; some sharpened skates. Some guys stretched; some guys got massages. Some guys changed gloves (Hull

Six—Times a Red Wing has won the Norris Trophy as the NHL's best defenseman:

Name	Season
Red Kelly	1953–1954
Paul Coffey	1995
Nicklas Lidstrom	2000–2001
Nicklas Lidstrom	2001–2002
Nicklas Lidstrom	2002–2003
Nicklas Lidstrom	2005–2006

went through eight pairs); some guys didn't (Shanahan used the same pair the whole game). Although many players changed T-shirts, no one asked for a new sweater.

"You try to dry everything off as much as possible, so you're going out there a little bit lighter," Shanahan said.

The Wings downed water, energy drinks, and Pedialyte, which was designed for sick children but is great for professional athletes because it has a lot of electrolytes and is absorbed quickly.

"I've given it to my little girl when she's gotten sick, and now we've found another use for it," center Kris Draper said. "It's strange how these things work out, but if we should win the Stanley Cup, maybe we should pour Pedialyte in there before any champagne."

The Wings hadn't had a meal since 1:30 PM or a snack since 4:30, so they ate bananas, sliced oranges, and energy bars.

"You try to eat what you can," Draper said. "You don't want to think about getting tired. You don't want your mind to start wandering in that direction. All we kept saying was, 'Look at where we are, how close we are to our ultimate goal. If you're tired at all, just think of that. Think of the big picture, not that we're going into a third overtime or whatever.'"

Carolina forward Jaroslav Svoboda had a chance early.

"I was kind of holding my breath a little bit," Yzerman said.

Both teams tried to catch their breath.

"Everybody was feeling it a little bit," Yzerman said. "It was basically one burst of energy and head right to the bench."

Duchesne took a puck in the mouth. He was missing six teeth—two natural, four from a bridge—but he missed only one shift.

"I've still got my bottom teeth, so I figure I'm all right," he said. "Besides, the guys said I looked better than I did before."

Then center Igor Larionov, the 41-year-old, the NHL's oldest player, the Dick Clark of hockey, who chewed on fruits and vegetables, who eschewed red meat, who said his secret was two glasses of wine every night, took a pass from forward Tomas Holmstrom. He stick-handled past diving defender Bates Battaglia. With defenseman Mathieu Dandenault in front, he backhanded the puck over Irbe and into the roof of the net at 14:47, becoming the oldest player ever to score in the Finals, ending the third-longest Finals game ever, giving the Wings a 3–2 victory and 2–1 series lead.

It was about 1:15 AM.

"I think this is the biggest goal of my career," said Larionov, who had never scored a playoff overtime goal before. "It's obviously huge for me."

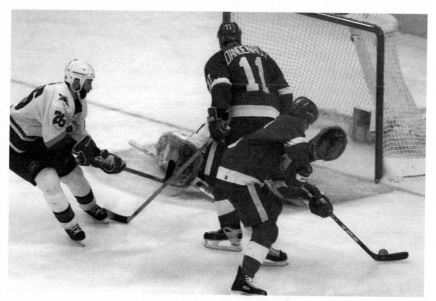

It was the third-longest Stanley Cup Finals game ever, and it was the NHL's oldest player who ended it. Igor Larionov, 41, gave the Red Wings a 3–2 victory over Carolina with a backhand shot 14:47 minutes into the third overtime of Game 3 in 2002.

TOP TEN

Red Wings Playoff Goaltending Records in Order of Wins

		Games	Record	GAA
1.	Terry Sawchuk	84	47–37	2.51
2.	Chris Osgood	68	38–25	2.16
3.	Mike Vernon	42	30–12	2.08
4.	Harry Lumley	54	24–30	2.26
5.	John Mowers	32	19–13	2.45
6.	Dominik Hasek	23	16–7	1.86
7.	Greg Stefan	30	12–17	3.53
8.	Norm Smith	12	9–2t	1.28
	Glen Hanlon	18	9–6t	2.58
	Roger Crozier	23	9–12t	2.59
	Tim Cheveldae	25	9–15t	3.00

"I have always thought that youth and enthusiasm will take you only so far," Hull said. "I said to Iggy after the game, 'I'd rather be old and smart than young and dumb any day.'"

"We're the oldest team in the league, and we had the oldest player go out and dance around a couple of guys like it was the first shift of the game," Shanahan said. "It's just a big relief to our entire team. We had so many chances that I think relief was part of the feeling."

The Wings celebrated. The Hurricanes deflated.

"There's no question that they're a great team, but . . . but it just looks like they have a way of getting the right break at the right time," Carolina forward Jeff O'Neill said. "Just when you think you might have them—bam!—they get what they need. I mean, we were a minute or so away from leading this series, 2–1, and then . . ."

Bam!

The full impact of fatigue didn't hit the Wings until they were on the bus or back at the hotel. They had a meal around 2:00 AM.

"We weren't even sure if the hotel was going to keep the food for us, but they did," Draper said.

There was pasta, pizza, chicken, salads—all kinds of stuff.

"The food was meant to be eaten about two or three hours earlier," forward Kirk Maltby said. "It was actually not bad. The chicken parm was pretty good. To their credit, they kept the food warm. It didn't go stale."

How was the atmosphere?

"Pretty quiet," Draper said.

"And content," Olausson said.

One by one, the players went to their rooms and tried to unwind. Many watched some World Cup soccer.

"Some guys I'm sure had a beer," Maltby said.

Maltby turned off his television, and although he was exhausted, he tossed and turned for 30 or 45 minutes before falling asleep between 4:30 and 5:00 AM.

"Your mind is racing," he said. "You're thinking about all the things that happened in the course of the game. It's hard to get to sleep when you're thinking about that kind of stuff. You're telling yourself to sleep, sleep, sleep. But every time you try to stop thinking about it, you just think about it more."

Needless to say, after playing 114 minutes and 47 seconds of hockey, neither team practiced the next day. Some players slept in as late as 1:00 PM.

Although he wasn't a big coffee drinker, when Lidstrom walked into an afternoon news conference, the first thing he did was grab a cup.

Decaf?

"No way," he said.

IF ONLY . . . Nicklas Lidstrom hadn't been so bland, he might not have waited so long to win the Norris Trophy as the NHL's best defenseman. Lidstrom was smooth and steady on the ice, and he was quiet and unassuming off the ice. Those are good qualities, but they don't attract the attention of the writers who vote for the award. Lidstrom was runner-up for the Norris three consecutive years before 2001–2003, when he became the first since Bobby Orr to win it three consecutive years. Lidstrom won it again in 2006.

Out on Top

Scotty Bowman retired the way he coached—by doing the unexpected.

He left the bench as the clock counted down on Game 5 of the 2002 Finals and went to put on his skates. When the final horn sounded, the confetti fell, and his players leapt into a happy heap around Dominik Hasek, celebrating the 3–1 victory that brought them the Stanley Cup, he skated out to join them, as he had done in 1997.

There was nothing more to accomplish. The Red Wings had 10 Cups—more than all but two teams, the Montreal Canadiens and the Toronto Maple Leafs—and so did he. He had one in the front office, and he had a record nine behind the bench, one more than his mentor, Toe Blake, who had won seven of his eight when you had to survive only two rounds, not four. Bowman held every important coaching record by far: five decades, 30 seasons, 2,141 regular-season games, 1,244 regular-season victories, 353 playoff games, 223 playoff victories, and on and on.

And so he found owner Mike Ilitch amid the throng, gave him a hug, and whispered in his ear: "Mike, it's time. The time is right now. It's time to go."

Ilitch was surprised. Bowman was 68, but he was in great shape and showed no signs of slowing down. Sure, Bowman had dropped hints during the finals: in a news conference before Game 3, a reporter asked if he would take some time after the series to think about his future, and Bowman said he already had made a decision, refusing to elaborate. In another news conference, a reporter asked about the possible labor stoppage in 2004, and Bowman said he wouldn't be around then. But if Bowman was anything, he was unpredictable. He had dropped hints in years past and still come back.

With the fans still roaring, some confetti still fluttering in the air, Marian Ilitch said to Bowman, "Wait. We have to talk about this." But there was nothing to talk about. When the Wings broke in the middle of their long season for the Olympics, Bowman and his family went to Florida. They spent time in the sun. Cold drinks, but no cold rinks. No practices. No games. No media. No pressure. And it was nice.

"I knew it would be four more years, the next Olympics, before I'd get to do that again, take time for myself in February, and that's when I decided," Bowman said. "I wasn't up to doing it anymore."

After taking a team photo with the 2002 Stanley Cup, Scotty Bowman skated into the sunset. He had nothing more to accomplish.

By the NUMBERS 11—The number of Red Wings who played in the 2002 Salt Lake Olympics. Brendan Shanahan and Steve Yzerman won gold for Canada; Chris Chelios and Brett Hull won silver for the United States; and Pavel Datsyuk, Sergei Fedorov, and Igor Larionov won bronze for Russia. Dominik Hasek represented the Czech Republic, and Tomas Holmstrom, Nicklas Lidstrom, and Fredrik Olausson played for Sweden. Not included is Henrik Zetterberg, who played for Sweden as a Detroit draft pick and joined the Wings in 2002–2003.

Bowman said he told maybe two or three people he could trust, because he didn't want to cause a distraction. He told his wife, Suella, of course. He even told New York Yankees manager Joe Torre and Yankees Hall of Famer Yogi Berra, whom he visited at spring training during the break. He didn't tell Ilitch or general manager Ken Holland, leaving them unprepared for his departure and with few candidates to replace him. But few criticized him for it, and just a handful criticized him for upstaging the team's ultimate moment.

The morning of Game 5, Bowman broke the news to his summertime neighbor in suburban Buffalo, CBC analyst and former coach Harry Neale.

"I'm retiring," Bowman told him, according to *Sports Illustrated.* "All the other times I considered it, I *thought* I knew I was ready. Now I *know* I know it."

"So what now?" Neale asked.

"Consultant," said Bowman, whose contract called for him to serve as one for three years after stepping down as coach. "Now I can go to the games and I don't have to win them."

Before the game, Bowman told his longtime associate Barry Smith that he would be retiring. Suella was sworn to secrecy, and she was under the impression the gag order wouldn't be lifted for a few days. But then the game ended, and Bowman told Ilitch. And Holland. And Steve Yzerman, his captain. And Brendan Shanahan, his favorite whipping boy. And Sergei Fedorov, his talented center (and occasional defenseman). And even Aaron Ward, who had become a Hurricane because they hadn't gotten along. He didn't get to everyone, but word spread quickly.

"I get down to the ice, and I find out that Scott had already told everyone," Suella said. "So when I find him, I ask him if I can finally answer questions now about this, and he said it was fine. I'm very happy for Scott, but I'm even happier for us and our family because now we'll have more time together to explore more things in life."

"My first reaction was probably shock," Yzerman said. "And then, just as quickly, I found myself to be very happy—happy for him because he's leaving on his own terms, having won the Stanley Cup in his last game. How can you have a better ending than that?"

"I was shocked," Shanahan said. "He's been so involved and so excited throughout the whole playoffs that I just thought, the way he was responding, 'This guy's going to go forever.' But I guess it makes sense now. He knew it was his last playoff, and that's why he soaked it all up."

"It's bittersweet," Brett Hull said. "To go out like this and to have the success he's had is so wonderful, but then to have it end is so sad. I feel as fortunate as anybody alive to say that he was my coach."

"I had a great conversation with the coach, finally," Fedorov said. "I said, 'It wasn't an easy road, but it was fun playing for you.' At times, it was very, very hard, but as long as we stick with the winning, that was the main goal. At times, he was asking more and more, and I have to adjust and do whatever Coach wants, and sometimes it didn't happen. But I think positive experiences happen more than negative. The way Scotty is, he's not really like that outside of the hockey circuit. I think he is a much, much better and wonderful person. I sense that. But he was a strong and tough coach. . . . He is the best coach ever. He can go out however he wants. He has nine championships."

TRIVIA

True or false: Scotty Bowman played for the Red Wings from 1934–1935 to 1939–1940.

Answers to the trivia questions are on pages 185–186.

Fedorov smiled.

"Maybe they should call it the Scotty Cup."

When commissioner Gary Bettman handed the Cup to Yzerman, Yzerman handed it right to Bowman.

"Without him," Yzerman said, pointing to the confetti on the ice, "none of this was possible. He taught me how to win. He taught us all that the only thing that matters is getting to this point, where the only goal, the only objective that you consider acceptable, is winning the Stanley Cup."

Bowman carried the Cup triumphantly. From resting his players down the stretch, to shuffling the lineup after those first two playoff losses, to telling stories before Game 7, he had been alert, not aloof. His last coaching performance had been one of his best.

"What a way for the greatest coach in the history of the sport to exit," Holland said. "He did an incredible job with all these egos and high-profile players. He got them all to buy into the team concept. He's the master."

Starstruck Stars

When the Red Wings went to the White House on November 8, 2002, it was the third time in six years they had been so honored as Stanley Cup champions. You would have thought meeting the president would have been old hat for them.

But it wasn't.

As George W. Bush shook hands with the players, he noticed some bruises and stitches around Kris Draper's left eye. Unaware Draper had been struck by a stick, he said, "I want to know what the other guy looks like."

Draper's mind raced. Eventually he blurted out, "Oh, you don't want to see *him*, Mr. President."

But by then, it was too late. Bush had moved on down the line.

"I turtled," Draper said, shaking his head and smiling. "His presence just rattles you. I'm pretty good with comebacks, but around Mr. President I wasn't as quick as I usually am."

The Wings were alternately the stars and the starstruck.

They had a police escort. They stepped off the bus on blocked-off Pennsylvania Avenue and signed autographs for fans, then stepped through the gate and had their names checked off a list by security. Even retired goaltender Dominik Hasek was there: he flew in just for the day from Prague, Czech Republic.

Sergei Fedorov wasn't an American citizen the last time the Wings visited. So as he stepped into the building, he pulled his blue U.S. passport from the left inside pocket of his sports coat, smiled, and said, "Part of the community now."

As Chris Chelios walked up to the entrance, a stern-looking secret service agent stopped him. Was there a problem? No. The agent pulled out a puck and asked Chelios for an autograph. Chelios obliged.

As Chelios walked down a hall, he looked out the window. He recalled visiting with the 1984 U.S. Olympic team—and Ronald Reagan shooting a puck on the team's goalie in the Rose Garden.

The Wings toured some rooms and signed autographs for government employees. With a handheld camcorder, Jason Williams taped Steve Yzerman taking pictures with some military police, then interviewed rookie Henrik Zetterberg.

"So," Williams said, "what do you think of this?"

"It's pretty nice," Zetterberg said.

"Are you nervous or scared about meeting the president?"

"No, no. I'm hanging out with you, so I'm OK."

The Wings assembled on a podium in the East Room, next to the Stanley Cup, between portraits of Dolley Madison and George Washington, before dignitaries that included Michigan senator Carl Levin and NHL commissioner Gary Bettman. Bush walked in right on time at 1:15 PM, shook hands with former coach Scotty Bowman, and gave a short speech.

George W. Bush brought the Red Wings to the White House to honor their 2002 title.

By the
NUMBERS

Nine—The number of potential Hall of Famers who played on the Red Wings' 2001–2002 Stanley Cup team. Chris Chelios, Sergei Fedorov, Dominik Hasek, Brett Hull, Igor Larionov, Nicklas Lidstrom, Luc Robitaille, Brendan Shanahan, and Steve Yzerman all seem destined for the Hall. And their coach, Scotty Bowman, has already been in the Hall for more than a decade.

A former owner of the Texas Rangers, Bush ribbed Tigers and Wings owner Mike Ilitch: "It just goes to prove it's easier to win in hockey than in baseball."

He praised Bowman for having his name on the Cup 10 times: "Obviously, he knows what he's doing. Gets all those ruffians skating in the same direction."

He commented on the Wings' roster, which had several all-time greats but only one American-born player, Chelios: "Doesn't look like a Hall of Fame ballot to me. It looks like the United Nations.

"I think it's a remarkable feat that you've got all these stars from different parts of the world, all aiming in the same direction," Bush said. "Darren McCarty put it this way: 'A lot of us were trying to get it back. Some guys were trying to do it for the first time. The bottom line is, we're all fighting to do it together.' And I appreciate that spirit. I think it's a good example for a lot of people who live in America."

McCarty couldn't believe the president quoted him.

"I've had some cool stuff happen to me in my life," he said. "That's right up there."

Yzerman couldn't believe it, either.

"Is that what this world has come to?" he joked.

Captain Comeback

In the commotion after the Red Wings won the 2002 Stanley Cup, with confetti still falling from the Joe Louis Arena rafters, captain Steve Yzerman said, "What do you think would happen if I announced my retirement right now?"

No one would have blamed him if he had.

It would have been a fitting finale to a Hall of Fame career: in a matter of months, he had won an Olympic gold medal for Canada and his third Cup for the Wings, and he had done it at age 37—despite unspeakable hardship.

His right knee was wrecked. He tore his posterior cruciate ligament in 1988 and didn't have it reconstructed. He wore away his cartilage over the years until bone ground against bone. Two games into the 2002 play-offs, the Wings weren't sure he could go on—but he went on, leading them on and off the ice, although he needed constant treatment, took countless injections, had trouble scaling the steps up to the team plane, and hardly left his home or hotel rooms.

Walking hurt. Even standing hurt. The knee ached all the time.

"He's a freak of nature," said John Wharton, the Wings' trainer at the time, who learned to worry mostly about Yzerman's swelling and range of motion. "I think he has a different nervous system than the rest of us. I don't think he processes pain."

But Yzerman had no intention of retiring. He was to make a comeback in which he would display the qualities that made him a legend.

Yzerman had his postseason physical June 18, 2002, and team ortho-pedist David Collon made a couple of appointments for June 24. That day, Collon, Yzerman, and trainer Piet Van Zant flew to New York and Pittsburgh in a private plane to see two specialists. Both recommended

Despite a wrecked right knee, Steve Yzerman was able to lift the 2002 Stanley Cup alongside his daughter Isabella.

IF ONLY . . . the Red Wings had gotten the man they really wanted in the 1983 draft, they wouldn't have had the Captain. With the fourth pick, the Wings hoped to take Pat LaFontaine, an outstanding player who happened to have grown up in the Detroit area. But the New York Islanders nabbed LaFontaine with the third pick. Although LaFontaine had a Hall of Fame career, he wasn't the player the Wings settled for, Steve Yzerman.

an osteotomy, a procedure that realigns the knee to redistribute weight, a procedure usually performed on elderly people with degenerative bone disease—a procedure that had never been done on a professional athlete.

The next week, Yzerman flew to Birmingham, Alabama, to get a third opinion from William Clancy, a renowned specialist who had known Yzerman and his knee for years. Yzerman said Clancy weighed the pros and cons of an osteotomy and PCL reconstruction; Van Zant said Clancy recommended a PCL reconstruction. Clancy told Yzerman to see one more man: Peter Fowler.

So the following week—nearing mid-July now—Yzerman drove to London, Ontario. Fowler, a 64-year-old who would have an osteotomy himself in a few months, recommended one for Yzerman. Fowler said the goal was Yzerman doing daily tasks without pain; returning to hockey would be a bonus.

"It came down to what was the best thing for my knee, number one, and then what's going to give me the best chance of playing again," Yzerman said.

Yzerman spoke with Clancy, and Clancy conferred with Fowler. Van Zant said there was some discussion about doing a PCL reconstruction on top of an osteotomy, but that would have kept Yzerman out for a year, and at this point in his career, that wasn't desirable. Surgery was scheduled. Yzerman wore a brace that simulated the effects of an osteotomy, and he was able to enjoy some of the summer.

But, Van Zant said, "there was definitely trepidation." No one knew how much the osteotomy would reduce the pain. No one knew how much function Yzerman would regain.

"I knew going in that this doesn't necessarily guarantee me playing any more, because there's some damage to the surface of the joint that you can't really do much about," Yzerman said. "Everyone was up front about that."

Fowler rearranged Yzerman's knee—which probably will need to be replaced someday—August 2. Within three weeks, Yzerman was on a stationary bike, slowly pedaling without resistance. On October 30, to most everyone's surprise, he was on the ice already, slowly circling without equipment.

Three or four or more hours a day he worked. The bike. StairMaster. Weights. Everything but the agility drills his knee couldn't—can't, and likely never will be able to—handle. At first, he struggled and thought, "God, this better get better, or I'm going to be in trouble." But eventually he progressed to the point where he overcame that doubt. He was patient, having been through all too many rehabilitations, knowing he had to wait until the time was right, and he said he didn't detest rehab. He is an exercise addict, and he pushed himself by tracking his progress minutely.

"I'd try to reach a level and go to another one," Yzerman said. "You've got to have goals, or else you just go through the motions."

The Wings wondered and worried. As Van Zant said, many of them wouldn't try to play under the circumstances—wouldn't even think about trying.

"When you saw how he was struggling in the weight room and how he was struggling on the ice," forward Kris Draper said, "you would kind of think, 'Is he going to be able to come back?'"

But if they doubted him, they didn't doubt him for long. He had dragged them through that first-round playoff series against Vancouver on that knee, hadn't he?

"You realize the kind of person that Stevie is," Draper said. "He's going to persevere."

Said senior vice president Jimmy Devellano, the man who drafted Yzerman fourth overall in 1983, "If anybody can come back from something like this, it would be Steve Yzerman. He just has a tremendously, tremendously strong will."

As Yzerman closed in on his comeback, the team began to feel his impact again. He was the longest-serving captain

TRIVIA

True or false: Wayne Gretzky and Mario Lemieux are the only NHL players who have produced more points in a season than the 155 Steve Yzerman did in 1988–1989.

Answers to the trivia questions are on pages 185–186.

in NHL history—he had worn the *C* for the Wings since he was 21 years old—and on February 14, 2003, the coaches let Yzerman run postpractice skating.

"We were down and back probably for a good 10 minutes," Draper said. "It was a good skate. He was the first one up, and whatever he did we had to do. Everyone kind of kept looking at him like, 'We played last night. We've got a game tomorrow.'"

The Wings beat Atlanta the next night, 6–2.

"Stevie's leadership, you can't simulate it," associate coach Barry Smith said. "You can't have somebody else take it over. His leadership on the ice and in the room is total."

Not long before he finally returned to the lineup on February 24 against Los Angeles—and finished the season and played all of 2003–2004—Yzerman sat on a bench in the Wings' weight room. Soaked with sweat between skating and riding a bike, he pondered the big question.

Why?

"I could have retired," he said. "But to be active and do things in the future, I needed the procedure for the longevity of my knee. I had to go through the rehab regardless of whether I wanted to play or not. To come back and play, that's the best motivation you could have to get strong again.

"But, you know, every time we win the Cup, someone says, 'Are you ready to retire?' And I'm like, 'No.' I'm 37. [Chris Chelios] is 41 and playing awesome. Igor [Larionov] is 42. I don't think I'll make it to 41 or 42, but I'm in no hurry to retire.

"I like playing. I have fun down here. We have a lot of fun down here on a day-to-day basis. You've got your whole life to be retired. If I can only do it for one more year, I'm going to do it.

"I guess I just haven't lost my desire to play. I still plan on going out on top—just not last year."

Yzerman didn't retire until July 2006. He was 41 years old.

The Long Road Back

They say the toughest jobs in Detroit sports are Lions quarterback and Red Wings goaltender. But the Lions never had a quarterback controversy quite like the goalie situation the Wings had in 2003–2004.

This soap opera had everything, from a clandestine meeting in Vienna, Austria; to a temper tantrum in St. Paul, Minnesota; to a long drive from Cleveland, Ohio, to Buffalo, New York, in a rented Chevy Cavalier.

Curtis Joseph joined the Wings in July 2002, after the Wings won the Stanley Cup and Dominik Hasek retired. It was hard for Joseph because he had to leave his hometown of Toronto. It was so hard, in fact, that he wept at his farewell news conference and said if the Wings didn't win the Cup, he hoped the Maple Leafs did.

It would only get harder.

Joseph never seemed to fit in his first season. He watched the banner-raising at the home opener, but when his teammates received their Cup rings at a dinner at the Fox Theatre, he didn't go. When the team went to the White House, he went, too, but as President George W. Bush spoke, he stood off to the side.

"Not being a part of it, that was a little bit different," he said.

Hasek's shadow was inescapable. When Joseph visited Children's Hospital of Michigan, the Wings' 2001–2002 highlight video was playing on a large screen in a room where a bunch of kids were, and as Joseph signed autographs, he could hear the announcer: "What a save by Hasek!" Joseph was constantly compared to his predecessor.

Things did not go well. Joseph didn't play in his return to Toronto, got pulled on Long Island, and clashed with coach Dave Lewis. The final

Curtis Joseph left his hometown of Toronto to replace Dominik Hasek in Detroit, hoping to win his first Stanley Cup. Things didn't go as planned.

straw was the playoffs. The Wings were swept by Anaheim. Although the Wings scored only six goals in the series, Joseph took a lot of the blame, because he had allowed some bad goals at bad times.

Hasek made noise about coming back starting in May 2003—and the Wings listened. Lewis even flew to Vienna that June just to spend half a day with Hasek.

"Mutually we felt it was a good idea to meet," Lewis said at the time. "He's typical Dominik. He looks the same as he did when I saw him the first time. No, he did look a little different. He had a tan."

The Wings signed Hasek, intending to trade Joseph. But for a variety of reasons, they were unable to make a deal, and Hasek and Joseph had to share the same dressing room. Aside from a quick handshake and some small talk, they didn't speak to each other. Their lockers were separated by the locker of goaltender Manny Legace, who joked he was "Jimmy Buffer."

"We cannot be both in the net," Hasek said in his heavy Czech accent, "so it's a little bit complicated."

The situation came to a head in November. At a morning skate at Minnesota, Joseph came onto the ice with his sweater inside out so the crest couldn't be seen, making him a man without a team. This was a major break from the Code. The coaches weren't sure what to do. Confront him? Kick him off the ice? Well, a coach confronted him, and there were some heated words.

Soon afterward, Joseph was pulled after allowing three goals on nine shots to lowly Washington. It was supposed to be his last game as a Wing. He was put on waivers, and after he cleared, he was sent to the minors—to the Wings' American Hockey League affiliate, Grand Rapids. But he never played a game for the Griffins.

IF ONLY . . . a labor dispute hadn't wiped out the 2004–2005 NHL season, the Red Wings might have had a shot at another Stanley Cup. The Wings would have had an all-star cast yet again—from Chris Chelios and Nicklas Lidstrom to Brendan Shanahan and Steve Yzerman. Young players like Pavel Datsyuk and Henrik Zetterberg were ready to take another step.

Five—Times a Red Wing has won the Vezina Trophy as the NHL's top goaltender:

Name	Season
Norm Smith	1936–1937
John Mowers	1942–1943
Terry Sawchuk	1951–1952
Terry Sawchuk	1952–1953
Terry Sawchuk	1954–1955

Hasek aggravated a nagging groin injury in a game December 8. The night of December 9, Joseph was playing cards at the back of the team bus as the Griffins made the 300-mile trip to Cleveland for a game against the Barons. He got a call from associate coach Barry Smith. Yes, the Wings hadn't wanted him. But now, they needed him.

The bus pulled up to the hotel.

"Fortunately," Joseph said, "there was a Hertz Rent A Car across the street."

Hertz had only one car left—a Chevy Cavalier. So Joseph, a 36-year-old All-Star with an $8 million salary, the highest-paid goaltender in the game, did what he had to do. He rented it, jammed his equipment in the back, and drove 200 miles to Buffalo with a passenger—19-year-old rookie Jiri Hudler, who was also getting called back up to the NHL.

The only clothing Joseph had was the sweat suit he was wearing. He hadn't packed much, because he thought he was going to be gone for only one game. Hudler didn't speak English very well, but that didn't really matter because he fell asleep. When Joseph pulled up to his second hotel, it had been dark for hours.

"It was a long day for him," Lewis said.

And yet the next night, Joseph started his first game in any league since the Washington debacle, and he made 23 saves in a 7–2 victory over the Sabres.

Asked if the situation were his worst nightmare, he said, "I would say it's a year of uncertainty—uncertainty for myself and my family—

and any time you go through uncertainty, that is something you have to challenge yourself with. Certainly it is a challenge, but you rise to the occasion."

Joseph was back to stay. Hasek never played another game for the Wings.

Until he came back to Detroit again in August 2006, at least.

Stanley Cups

The Red Wings have won 10 Stanley Cups, the most of any American franchise. Only the Montreal Canadiens (23) and the Toronto Maple Leafs (13) have won more.

1936

In its 10th season in the NHL, after some good times and some hard times, the franchise finally found a real foothold with its first championship. The Wings finished fourth—or last—in the American Division and missed the playoffs in 1934–1935. But they roared back in 1935–1936 and won the division and the Cup.

General manager and coach Jack Adams had a top scoring line in Larry Aurie, Herbie Lewis, and Marty Barry and a top goalie in Normie Smith. He also had great players like forward Syd Howe and defenseman Ebbie Goodfellow.

The Wings opened the playoffs with a historic victory, a six-overtime, 1–0 marathon over the defending champions, the Montreal Maroons. Mud Bruneteau, a bench-warming rookie, hopped onto the ice for his first shift, and his fresh legs helped him put an end to it at 2:25 AM. It was the longest game of the century.

Smith shut out the Maroons in Game 2, too, and allowed only one goal in Game 3 as the Wings swept the best-of-five series. Smith went 248 minutes and 32 seconds without allowing a puck past him.

Next up were the finals against the Toronto Maple Leafs. The Wings won the series, 3–1, and their only loss had come in overtime. The Cup came after the Tigers won their first World Series, the Lions won their first NFL title, and Joe Louis rose to boxing prominence. Detroit became known as the "City of Champions."

1937

The Wings became the first American team to win back-to-back Cups. They had largely the same cast as in 1936, but they needed some help from a new face and a circus to get the job done.

Aurie scored 23 regular-season goals, becoming the first Red Wing to lead the league in that category. But a broken ankle kept him out of the playoffs. Defenseman Doug Young, the captain, sat out with a broken leg. Smith and Goodfellow also were hampered by injuries.

The Wings squeaked past the Montreal Canadiens in the first round, winning the fifth and final game of the series on a triple-overtime goal by Hec Kilrea. Few gave them a chance in the Finals against the rested New York Rangers, and they lost the opener in Manhattan, 5–1.

But then the circus bumped the series out of Madison Square Garden. The final four games had to be played at Olympia Stadium.

And then goaltender Earl Robertson, a rookie up from the farm, led the Wings to victory. He won Game 2, 4–2. He lost Game 3, but by a 1–0 score. Then he posted back-to-back shutouts in Games 4 and 5.

Adams was so overwhelmed by the victory he fainted in the dressing room.

1943

The Wings made the Finals in 1941 but were swept by the Boston Bruins. They made it back in 1942 and took a 3–0 series lead, but they blew it—something no other team has done in the Finals—in large part because Adams went after a referee after Game 4 and was suspended. They made it for the third year in a row in 1943, and that time they won their third Cup.

The league shrank to six teams in 1942–1943—Boston, Chicago, Detroit, Montreal, New York, and Toronto—so the Wings won the first Cup of what became known as the "Original Six" era.

Goodfellow was a link to the team's earlier glory, and Sid Abel and "Black" Jack Stewart were links to the glory to come. Syd Howe was a star.

Series were now best-of-seven. The Wings beat the Leafs in the first round,

TRIVIA

True or false: only twice has a hockey player's ultimate dream come true—with an overtime goal in Game 7 of the Stanley Cup Finals—and both times it was a Red Wing who put the puck into the net.

Answers to the trivia questions are on pages 185–186.

141

4–2, then faced the Bruins in the Finals. They did to the Bs what the Bs had done to them two years before, winning in a sweep. Goaltender Johnny Mowers, who won the Vezina Trophy as the league's top goal-tender in the regular season, shut out Boston in the final two games.

Players and fans celebrated on the train from Boston back to Detroit, putting the Cup in a men's room, filling it with beer, and serving the beer in paper cups.

1950

Again, the Wings followed back-to-back Finals losses with a Finals victory. This was the first Cup of the Gordie Howe era, but Howe appeared in only one playoff game, the opener, in which he suffered a severe head injury.

Adams was now just the general manager. Tommy Ivan was the coach, and he had a lineup of legends, including Abel, Howe, Stewart, Ted Lindsay, Red Kelly, and Marcel Pronovost. Lindsay led the league in scoring during the regular season with 78 points—23 goals and 55 assists.

Both series went seven games, and both Game 7s went to overtime. The Wings beat Toronto in the first round. They faced New York in the Finals, and as in 1937, they were helped when the circus kicked hockey out of Madison Square Garden. Game 1 was in Detroit. Games 2 and 3 were in Toronto. The rest of the series was in Detroit.

The Rangers' Don Raleigh set a record that would remain untouched until 1993 when he scored two OT goals in the Finals, but he didn't have the magic touch when it mattered most, in the first Game 7 overtime in Finals history.

Pete Babando went from benchwarmer to hero much the same way Bruneteau did in 1936, scoring on a backhand shot 8:31 into the second overtime, ending the game—and the season—at 12:14 AM.

1952

This might have been the greatest Detroit team of all time—one of the greatest NHL teams of all time.

The Wings ran away with the regular-season title, finishing 22 points ahead of the next best team, Montreal. Howe won his first Hart

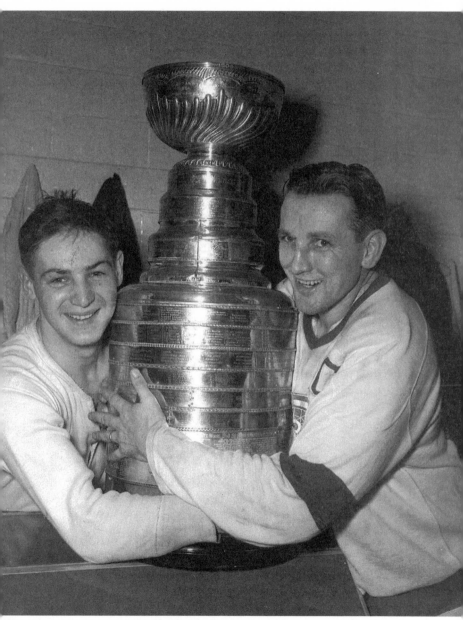

Terry Sawchuk (left) and Sid Abel hug the Stanley Cup in 1952. That might have been Detroit's best team: the Red Wings went 8–0 in the playoffs.

Memorial Trophy as the league's most valuable player. He led the league in scoring for the second straight year with 86 points. Lindsay was second with 69.

You needed eight victories to win the Cup in those days. Well, the Wings needed only eight games, because they won them all. They swept the Leafs in the first round. Then they swept the Canadiens. And they felt like they would have kept winning had they played all summer.

Goaltender Terry Sawchuk, who was so good in the regular season that he won his first Vezina, continued to dominate in the playoffs. He didn't allow a goal on home ice, pitching two shutouts in each series, and allowed only five goals total.

1954

The Wings had another dominant regular season, like the one they had in 1952. Howe won a fourth-straight scoring title with 81 points. Lindsay continued to star. Red Kelly won the first Norris Trophy as the league's top defenseman—appropriate, considering the award was named for the late Wings owner James Norris. Glen Skov, Marty Pavelich, and Tony Leswick formed an early day Grind Line.

But they won the Cup thanks to a Game 7 overtime goal by an unlikely hero, as they had in 1950. The Wings beat the Leafs in the first round, then met the Canadiens in the finals. The Wings took a 3–1 series lead, but the Habs fought back and forced a Game 7.

In OT, Leswick, the checker, who was only 5'7", 160 pounds or so, lifted a lazy shot toward the Montreal net. Defenseman Doug Harvey tried to knock down the puck so he could play it, but somehow the puck went off his glove and over the goalie's shoulder.

The old Olympia roared. The Canadiens were so stunned and upset, they marched off the ice without shaking the Wings' hands.

1955

The Wings had a tumultuous season in 1954–1955, but they managed to win their fourth Cup in six years. That gave them seven Cups total. Only the Leafs had won as many.

Jimmy Skinner replaced Ivan as coach. Howe missed some games because of a shoulder injury and didn't win the scoring title. The team

IF ONLY . . . Jack Adams hadn't gotten so upset about some calls in the 1942 Stanley Cup Finals against Toronto, the Red Wings might have won another championship. Adams chased referee Mel Harwood into the officials' dressing room after Game 4 and was suspended for the rest of the series. The Wings became the first team to blow a 3–0 lead in the playoffs.

dealt with the Richard Riot in Montreal. Still, the Wings won their seventh straight regular-season title.

They swept the Leafs in the first round of the playoffs, then met the Canadiens in the Finals for the third time in four years. The Wings won the series in seven games, and they seemed capable of winning Cup after Cup after Cup. This time, humbled in defeat, the Canadiens shook hands.

But Adams, who had kept his team intact after the 1936 and 1937 Cups and watched it slip, traded away half the team. The Wings made the Finals five times in the next 11 years, but they didn't win their next Cup for 42 years.

1997

For years, the Red Wings were so bad they were known as the Dead Things. Slowly, they came back to life.

Scotty Bowman took over as coach in 1993–1994 and eventually molded Steve Yzerman and company into champions. The Wings lost in the first round in 1994. They made the Finals in 1995 but were swept by the New Jersey Devils. They were the favorites to win the 1996 Cup, after winning a record 62 regular-season games, but they were upset by the Colorado Avalanche in the conference finals.

The Wings didn't even win their division in 1996–1997. In fact, they finished with 37 fewer points than they had the season before. But all that mattered was the playoffs. All that mattered was the Cup.

Bowman put veteran Mike Vernon in the net for the playoffs instead of Chris Osgood, and Vernon won the Conn Smythe Trophy as the play-offs' most valuable player. The Wings beat the St. Louis Blues in six games, swept the Mighty Ducks of Anaheim, avenged their loss to Colorado in six games, then swept the Philadelphia Flyers.

Detroit became Hockeytown.

1998

Six days after the 1997 Cup, defenseman Vladimir Konstantinov and team masseur Sergei Mnatsakanov were seriously injured in a limousine accident, muting the celebration. The Wings sewed patches on their sweaters that said "Believe" in English and Russian, then set out to win one for their fallen comrades.

Again, the Wings didn't even win their division. But again, all that mattered was the playoffs. All that mattered was the Cup. The Wings downed the Phoenix Coyotes, the St. Louis Blues, and the Dallas Stars in six games apiece, then swept the Washington Capitals.

When NHL commissioner Gary Bettman handed the Cup to Yzerman, who had won the Conn Smythe this time, Yzerman placed it on the lap of Konstantinov, who had been brought onto the ice in a wheelchair.

Clenching a cigar in his mouth and wearing a championship hat on his head, Konstantinov, who had suffered brain damage in the accident, raised an index finger. Even without their Norris-caliber defenseman in the lineup, the Wings were number one again.

2002

The Wings seemed to be slipping when they lost to the Los Angeles Kings in the first round of the 2001 playoffs, after losing to Colorado in the second round in 1999 and 2000. They had to do something.

General manager Ken Holland acquired goaltender Dominik Hasek, then left wing Luc Robitaille, then right wing Brett Hull, all in the same summer. With Yzerman, Chris Chelios, Sergei Fedorov, Igor Larionov, Nicklas Lidstrom, and Brendan Shanahan, the Wings had nine potential Hall of Famers.

IF ONLY . . . Boston hadn't traded Marty Barry to Detroit in 1935, the Red Wings might not have won back-to-back Stanley Cups in 1936 and 1937. Barry became the Wings' leading scorer in 1935–1936 with 40 points and in 1936–1937 with 44 points. He led the Wings in scoring again in 1938–1939 with 41 points.

Yes, they were old. But they were talented, smart, savvy, experienced—and they put on a helluva show. They jumped out to a 22–3–1–1 start and ran away with the regular season. They were so far ahead at the end, they rested some players, fell out of their groove, and fell behind in their first-round series with the Vancouver Canucks, 2–0.

But they got it together in time, beat the Canucks in six, the Blues in five, the Avs in seven, and the Carolina Hurricanes in five. And when it was over, Bowman had nine Cups as a coach, breaking the record his mentor, Toe Blake, had set with Montreal.

Right there on the ice, amid the celebration, Bowman announced his retirement.

All-Time Teams

First Team

Left Wing: Ted Lindsay

Lindsay has said he hated everyone he played against and everyone he played against hated him. Although he was only 5'8", 163 pounds, he not only didn't back down from his opponents, he went after them. He earned the nicknames "Scarface," because of the hundreds of stitches he took over his career, and "Terrible Ted," because of all the penalty minutes he racked up.

"I had the idea that I had to beat up everybody in the league," Lindsay said. "I'm still not convinced it wasn't a good idea."

His attitude sometimes overshadowed his skill, which was considerable. In 1949–1950, he became the first Red Wing to win the Art Ross Trophy as the NHL's leading scorer, with 78 points. He remains the only Wing to do it other than Gordie Howe, and he was runner-up three times.

Nothing illustrated Lindsay's lack of fear better than the first round of the 1952 playoffs. The Wings were leading the Toronto Maple Leafs, 2–0, when someone threatened to shoot Lindsay and Howe if they took the ice at Maple Leafs Gardens.

"We were in the locker room joking about it before the game," Lindsay said in Paul Harris's *Heroes of Hockeytown from A to Z.* "Guys were saying, 'Hey, this guy is liable to be a bad shot, so don't skate too close to us in warm-ups.'"

Needless to say, Lindsay and Howe played. Lindsay scored the tying goal in the third period and the game winner in overtime. As the crowd booed, he skated to center ice, turned his stick around, held it like a gun, and pretended to shoot.

IF ONLY . . . Jack Adams hadn't traded Terry Sawchuk to Boston in 1955, he wouldn't have had to trade Johnny Bucyk to the Bruins to get Sawchuk back two years later. Bucyk went on to score 545 goals in 21 seasons with the Bruins and made the Hall of Fame.

"I don't know what made me do it, but there were about 500 Red Wing fans there and about 16,000 Leafs fans," Lindsay said in Harris's book. "All of the Leafs fans were booing because we had won, of course, but when I went to center ice and did that, they started to clap. They must have figured, 'Well, this guy Lindsay has a sense of humor.'"

Lindsay, a leader who captained the Wings, wasn't afraid of battling management, either. He didn't join the NHL until general manager and coach Jack Adams gave him a no-minor-leagues clause in his contract. Despite his on-ice relations with his fellow players, he was able to get them together to try to form an NHL players' association.

That got him shipped from his beloved Wings to the Chicago Black Hawks.

"I played for three years in Chicago," Lindsay said in Harris's book. "But I had a Red Wing tattooed on my forehead, my backside, and on my heart."

Lindsay retired in 1960 at age 34 and spent four years working on his automotive plastics company in Detroit. But he returned in 1964 for one more season with the Wings—Sid Abel, his old Production Line mate, had replaced Adams as the GM—and he was still good enough to produce 28 points and still nasty enough to rack up 173 penalty minutes. He later served as the Wings' general manager and coach.

"He was a mean sucker," Wings great Bill Gadsby said in Rich Kincaide's *The Gods of Olympia Stadium: Legends of the Detroit Red Wings.* "He was one of the meanest guys who ever played in the NHL, Ted Lindsay. He'd put that stick right in your mouth. I saw him do some funny things when he came back in '64. Guys would take a run at him; they'd have to come through that lumber before they got to him, I'll tell you that."

TRIVIA

Who holds the Red Wings record for most goals in a game?

A. Syd Howe

B. Gordie Howe

C. Mark Howe

D. Sergei Fedorov

Answers to the trivia questions are on pages 185–186.

149

Ted Lindsay Statistics

	Regular Season				Playoffs			
	GP	G	A	Pts.	GP	G	A	Pts.
1944–1945	45	17	6	23	14	2	0	2
1945–1946	47	7	10	17	5	0	1	1
1946–1947	59	27	15	42	5	2	2	4
1947–1948	60	33	19	52	10	3	1	4
1948–1949	50	26	28	54	11	2	6	8
1949–1950	69	23	55	78	13	4	4	8
1950–1951	67	24	35	59	6	0	1	1
1951–1952	70	30	39	69	8	5	2	7
1952–1953	70	32	39	71	6	4	4	8
1953–1954	70	26	36	62	12	4	4	8
1954–1955	49	19	19	38	11	7	12	19
1955–1956	67	27	23	50	10	6	3	9
1956–1957	70	30	55	85	5	2	4	6
1964–1965	69	14	14	28	7	3	0	3
Totals	862	335	393	728	123	44	44	88

Stanley Cup: 1950, 1952, 1954, 1955

NHL First All-Star Team: 1948, 1950, 1951, 1952, 1953, 1954, 1956, 1957

NHL Second All-Star Team: 1949

Art Ross Trophy: 1950

NHL All-Star Game: 1947, 1948, 1949, 1950, 1951, 1952, 1953, 1954, 1955, 1956, 1957

Hall of Fame

Center: Steve Yzerman

In the late eighties and early nineties, Yzerman scored 50 goals or more five times and more than 100 points six times. Perhaps only two players were more potent: Wayne Gretzky and Mario Lemieux. While Gretzky won the Hart Memorial Trophy as the NHL's most valuable player in 1989, Yzerman won the Lester B. Pearson Award as the NHL Players' Association's most outstanding player.

But then coach Scotty Bowman arrived. The league was becoming less wide-open, the Wings were becoming more well-rounded, and Bowman turned Yzerman from a one-way player into a two-way player, as he had done with the Montreal Canadiens' Jacques Lemaire in the seventies and the Pittsburgh Penguins' Ron Francis in the early nineties.

The evolution wasn't easy on Yzerman. The Wings considered trading him (though he had so much public support, the fans booed Bowman, the director of player personnel, because of it). His offensive production dropped. The Wings were swept by the New Jersey Devils in the 1995 finals, they had a banner regular season in 1995–1996 but lost in the Western Conference finals to the Colorado Avalanche, and he was haunted by the fact that he still wasn't a winner.

The *Detroit Free Press* reported this telling anecdote: once, Yzerman was on vacation in Las Vegas, and while he sat at a craps table, two guys recognized him. *Hey, it's Yzerman from the Red Wings!* They looked at the action, they looked at Yzerman, and one of them whispered, "We better

Detroit Red Wing Steve Yzerman became the 18th player in NHL history with 1,300 points after scoring a goal in the second period during a game against the Chicago Blackhawks on Sunday, January 5, 1997, in Chicago. Photo courtesy of AP Photo/Tim Boyle.

get away from here. There's no luck at this table." Yzerman said he "wanted to slug 'em." But he didn't.

After his first Stanley Cup, his game wasn't the only thing that had changed. Amid the spraying champagne, he said, "They always say, 'He's a good player, but he didn't win it.' And now they can't say that anymore. No matter what, they can't say it, you know?"

In 1997 Yzerman finished two votes shy of winning the Conn Smythe Trophy as the playoffs' MVP. In 1998, as he was closing on his Ontario cabin, once owned by the trophy's namesake, he did win it. In 2000 he won the Selke Trophy as the league's best defensive forward. In 1991 he was cut from a Canada Cup team; in 1998 and 2002 he made Olympic teams.

His stature grew more for his willingness to sacrifice than it ever had for his ability to score. He became known for his hot competitiveness, for his determination to win. He was the Wings' moral center. His teammates tried to follow his example on the ice, in the dressing room, in the weight room—and everywhere else. On the road, even if they weren't hanging out with him, they often would find out where he was going and what time he was coming back.

Yzerman didn't have the colorful personality of, say, Brendan Shanahan. His words had weight because of what he had accomplished but also because he spoke less than most. He had a dry sense of humor. He was moody and not always approachable. But he was without question the Wings' most popular player.

Alex Delvecchio and Gordie Howe were the only others to have played more than 1,000 games for the Wings, and the fans felt attached to him. With affection, having watched him since he was a teenager, a heartthrob with high cheekbones, they called him "Stevie" or "Stevie Y." With respect, having watched him grow into a man, a father of three daughters with a scarred, striking face, they called him "the Captain." He was the mayor of Hockeytown. Even after the Wings acquired Dominik Hasek, Brett Hull, and Luc Robitaille, their top-selling sweater was No. 19.

"People are always asking me, 'Who do you think are the great hockey players of all time?'" owner Mike Ilitch once said. "And I say they're the guys who can skate, shoot the puck, play defense, muck it up as rough as anybody, and not hang up at the blue line and cherry-pick. That's Steve Yzerman. He probably rivals Gordie Howe more than anybody I've ever seen."

Steve Yzerman Statistics

	Regular Season				Playoffs			
	GP	G	A	Pts.	GP	G	A	Pts.
1983–1984	80	39	48	87	4	3	3	6
1984–1985	80	30	59	89	3	2	1	3
1985–1986	51	14	28	42	–	–	–	–
1986–1987	80	31	59	90	16	5	13	18
1987–1988	64	50	52	102	3	1	3	4
1988–1989	80	65	90	155	6	5	5	10
1989–1990	79	62	65	127	–	–	–	–
1990–1991	80	51	57	108	7	3	3	6
1991–1992	79	45	58	103	11	3	5	8
1992–1993	84	58	79	137	7	4	3	7
1993–1994	58	24	58	82	3	1	3	4
1995	47	12	26	38	15	4	8	12
1995–1996	80	36	59	95	18	8	12	20
1996–1997	81	22	63	85	20	7	6	13
1997–1998	75	24	45	69	22	6	18	24
1998–1999	80	29	45	74	10	9	4	13
1999–2000	78	35	44	79	8	0	4	4
2000–2001	54	18	34	52	1	0	0	0
2001–2002	52	13	35	48	23	6	17	23
2002–2003	16	2	6	8	4	0	1	1
2003–2004	75	18	33	51	11	3	2	5
2005–2006	61	14	20	34	4	0	4	4
Totals	1,514	692	1,063	1,755	196	70	115	185

Stanley Cup: 1997, 1998, 2002

NHL All-Rookie Team: 1984

Pearson Award: 1989

Conn Smythe Trophy: 1998

NHL First All-Star Team: 2000

Selke Trophy: 2000

Masterton Trophy: 2003

NHL All-Star Game: 1984, 1988, 1989, 1990, 1991, 1992, 1993, 1997, 2000

Right Wing: Gordie Howe

Howe was arguably the best ever to play hockey. Period.

As great as Bobby Orr and Wayne Gretzky were, neither matched Howe's combination of scoring, toughness, intimidation, and longevity. Howe was neither artist nor innovator. He played raw hockey, old-time hockey, Detroit hockey, ripping wrist shots and exploding elbows like atom bombs.

Howe never needed the help of enforcers. He was his own policeman, one of the best in the game. He once skated past a heckler in the crowd and nicked the offender's nose with the blade of his stick, shutting him up. He often did much more than nick opponents when they dared challenge him. In 1959 Howe engaged in perhaps his most famous fight.

The New York Rangers that year promoted defenseman Lou Fontinato as the toughest player in hockey. New York–based *Look* magazine even presented a six-page picture spread on him, showing him flexing his muscles and looking mean. Whenever the Rangers played the Wings, Fontinato was on the ice with Howe.

"The idea was to work on me and distract me," Howe said in Richard Bak's *Detroit Red Wings: The Illustrated History.*

After a few altercations one night at Madison Square Garden, Howe got even.

"Red Kelly and Eddie Shack were in a fight behind our net, and I'm leaning on the net, watching it," Howe said in Bak's book. "Then I remembered a bit of advice from Lindsay: always be aware of who's out on the ice with you. I took a peek, and sure enough, there was Louis with his gloves off about 10 feet away. I truly thought he was going to sucker punch me. If he had, I'd have been over. I pretended I didn't see him, and when he swung, I just pulled my head aside. That honker of his was right there. I drilled it. It broke his nose a little bit."

A little bit? With one punch, Howe made a mess out of Fontinato's face and further solidified his reputation as the league's only one-man team. Even rival Maurice "Rocket" Richard, whom Howe felled with one punch in his first visit to the Montreal Forum in 1946, eventually admitted Howe's utter overall superiority.

"Sincerely, I have never seen a greater hockey player—I mean, a more complete player," Richard said. "Gordie Howe does everything and does it well."

Athletically, there was little Howe couldn't do. He was so strong from the waist up, he could outmuscle almost anyone. In any sport. He was a wicked golfer, booming balls off the tee. He once played with PGA champion Chick Harbert and outdrove him on every hole. One day, Cleveland Indians manager Lou Boudreau invited him to take batting practice before a game at Detroit's Briggs Stadium. After seeing two pitches, Howe drove the third into the left-field seats.

Howe spent some of his finest seasons playing with Lindsay and veteran captain Sid Abel as part of the Production Line, a scoring machine with a name that meshed well with Detroit's manufacturing image. The three were marvels to watch, taking long shifts of up to three minutes, crossing and criss-crossing in front of each other, banging the puck off a special spot of the Olympia Stadium boards to create scoring chances.

"Gordie would lead the charge down the right wing, and just after he crossed center ice, he'd fire the puck between the defensemen," center Murray Costello said in Bak's book. "If he hit the spot just right—and he was uncanny about hitting it—the puck came right out to the top of the left circle, and Lindsay would scoot in behind the defensemen and get a point-blank shot on goal."

Said Chicago star Bobby Hull, "I wish I was half the player Gordie was."

Gordie Howe Statistics

	Regular Season				Playoffs			
	GP	G	A	Pts.	GP	G	A	Pts.
1946–1947	58	7	15	22	5	0	0	0
1947–1948	60	16	28	44	10	1	1	2
1948–1949	40	12	25	37	11	8	3	11
1949–1950	70	35	33	68	1	0	0	0
1950–1951	70	43	43	86	6	4	3	7
1951–1952	70	47	39	86	8	2	5	7
1952–1953	70	49	46	95	6	2	5	7
1953–1954	70	33	48	81	12	4	5	9
1954–1955	64	29	33	62	11	9	11	20
1955–1956	70	38	41	79	10	3	9	12
1956–1957	70	44	45	89	5	2	5	7
1957–1958	64	33	44	77	4	1	1	2

	Regular Season				Playoffs			
	GP	G	A	Pts.	GP	G	A	Pts.
1958–1959	70	32	46	78	–	–	–	–
1959–1960	70	28	45	73	6	1	5	6
1960–1961	64	23	49	72	11	4	11	15
1961–1962	70	33	44	77	–	–	–	–
1962–1963	70	38	48	86	11	7	9	16
1963–1964	69	26	47	73	14	9	10	19
1964–1965	70	29	47	76	7	4	2	6
1965–1966	70	29	46	75	12	4	6	10
1966–1967	69	25	40	65	–	–	–	–
1967–1968	74	39	43	82	–	–	–	–
1968–1969	76	44	59	103	–	–	–	–
1969–1970	76	31	40	71	4	2	0	2
1970–1971	63	23	29	52	–	–	–	–
Totals	1,687	786	1,023	1,809	154	67	91	158

Stanley Cup: 1950, 1952, 1954, 1955

NHL Second All-Star Team: 1949, 1950, 1956, 1959, 1961, 1962, 1964, 1965, 1967

NHL First All-Star Team: 1951, 1952, 1953, 1954, 1957, 1958, 1960, 1963, 1966, 1968, 1969, 1970

Art Ross Trophy: 1951, 1952, 1953, 1954, 1957, 1963

Hart Memorial Trophy: 1952, 1953, 1957, 1958, 1960, 1963

NHL All-Star Game: 1948, 1949, 1950, 1951, 1952, 1953, 1954, 1955, 1957, 1958, 1959, 1960, 1961, 1962, 1963, 1964, 1965, 1967, 1968, 1969, 1970, 1971

Hall of Fame

Defense: Red Kelly

Kelly had one trait that was rare for defensemen of his era and another that was rare for defensemen of any era.

He could score. He rushed the puck into the offensive zone like no other defenseman did before Bobby Orr. He ranked in the top 10 in NHL scoring in 1950–1951, 1952–1953, and 1953–1954.

He was clean, too. Not only was he known for playing fair on the ice, but he was also known for not cursing—and not caring for anyone else cursing—on the ice or off it.

But that didn't mean he slacked off in his own end. That didn't mean he was soft. Because of his speed and positioning, Kelly was rarely beaten by opposing forwards. Because of his toughness, he played through all sorts of injuries.

No wonder, then, that Kelly won the first Norris Trophy as the league's best defenseman, in 1954, after becoming the first defenseman to win the Lady Byng Memorial Trophy for sportsmanship, gentlemanly conduct, and a high standard of playing ability, in 1951. He won two more Lady Byng Trophies as a Wing, in 1953 and 1954. He remains the only defenseman ever to win the award.

Kelly spent his first 12-plus seasons with the Wings, winning four Stanley Cups. He went on to play another seven-plus seasons as a center with the Toronto Maple Leafs, winning four more Cups, not to mention another Lady Byng. No player has won that many championships without also skating for the Montreal Canadiens.

But he never wanted to leave Detroit, and he had to be talked out of retiring to play for the Leafs.

Late in the 1958–1959 season, Kelly suffered a broken ankle when he was hit by a shot in practice. The Wings were struggling, and Kelly couldn't have done any more damage to himself. So when general manager Jack Adams and coach Sid Abel asked if he could play, he taped up the ankle and went out there. He didn't play well, because he couldn't turn to his left, but he played. The Wings missed the playoffs for the first time in his career.

As Kelly rehabilitated over the summer, people started saying his legs were shot.

"I'm seeing these reports and thinking, 'Well, the brass knows what's happened. What the hang?'" Kelly said in Rich Kincaide's *The Gods of Olympia Stadium: Legends of the Detroit Red Wings.* "'Why aren't they telling the reporters what happened to me?'"

By the NUMBERS **$8 million**—Amount Mike Ilitch paid for the down-and-out Red Wings in 1982. Twenty years later, after the team had won its third Stanley Cup in six years, *Forbes* magazine valued the franchise at $266 million—most in the NHL.

Kelly was good as new in 1959–1960. One day, when a Toronto reporter asked why he was playing better, Kelly revealed what had happened. The *Detroit Free Press* followed the story and printed the headline: Was Red Kelly Forced to Play on Broken Foot? The headline overplayed the story, but the damage was done.

Soon afterward, Adams told Kelly he had been traded to the New York Rangers with Billy McNeill for Bill Gadsby and Eddie Shack. Kelly was furious because he had done so much for the team, and he refused to report. NHL president Clarence Campbell told him he would be blacklisted; he resigned himself to retiring and working in the auto industry.

A little while later, the Leafs called Kelly and asked if he would be interested in playing for them. He flew to Toronto in disguise and under an assumed name to discuss it. He agreed, and a deal was done.

"I never thought I'd play anywhere but Detroit," Kelly said in Kincaide's book. "I can still hardly believe I didn't."

The rest is history. Kelly's father was classmates with Adams once upon a time, and after his son had gone on to have so much success with the Leafs, he ran into Adams at Maple Leaf Gardens.

"Isn't it funny how the Stanley Cup seems to follow that boy around?" he said to Adams.

From then on, whenever Adams saw Kelly's father, he went the other way.

Red Kelly Statistics

| | Regular Season | | | | Playoffs | | | |
	GP	G	A	Pts.	GP	G	A	Pts.
1947–1948	60	6	14	20	10	3	2	5
1948–1949	59	5	11	16	11	1	1	2
1949–1950	70	15	25	40	14	1	3	4
1950–1951	70	17	37	54	6	0	1	1
1951–1952	67	16	31	47	5	1	0	1
1952–1953	70	19	27	46	6	0	4	4
1953–1954	62	16	33	49	12	5	1	6
1954–1955	70	15	30	45	11	2	4	6
1955–1956	70	16	34	50	10	2	4	6
1956–1957	70	10	25	35	5	1	0	1
1957–1958	61	13	18	31	4	0	1	1

1958–1959	67	8	13	21	–	–	–	–
1959–1960	50	6	12	18	–	–	–	–
Totals	846	162	310	472	94	16	21	37

Stanley Cup: 1950, 1952, 1954, 1955

NHL Second All-Star Team: 1950, 1956

NHL First All-Star Team: 1951, 1952, 1953, 1954, 1955, 1957

Lady Byng Trophy: 1951, 1953, 1954

Norris Trophy: 1954

NHL All-Star Game: 1950, 1951, 1952, 1953, 1954, 1955, 1956, 1957, 1958, 1960

Hall of Fame

Defense: Nicklas Lidstrom

Lidstrom wasn't Mr. Emotion. He was thin, blond, with ice-blue eyes, and to find something truly colorful about him, you had to go to Vasteras, Sweden, where he played before Detroit, where he lived in the summer—and where he was part owner of an American-style sports bar, Bars and Stars.

When you thought of a Wings defenseman owning a sports bar back home, you thought of Chris Chelios, who owned Cheli's Chili Bar in Chicago and later in suburban Detroit. Cheli was a rabble-rouser, the kind of guy you envisioned cracking open a couple of cold ones. But Lidstrom? He never would have thought of rousing a rabble. He was the kind of guy you envisioned walking into a bar and saying, "Got milk?" Maybe he would go nuts and order a Magic, the energy drink he owned.

"Nick is relaxed, carefree," Bars and Stars employee Erik Soderlind said. "I ask him if he wants coffee, and he says, 'No, I'll get my own coffee.' I'm like, 'Sit! Sit! You're one of the best defensemen in the world!' He doesn't sit. Really, he's just a nice guy."

Bars and Stars had a drink named for his team and number, the Red Wing No. 5. It was a red mixture of booze and cranberry juice, served with an umbrella and some silver tinsel. Asked about the drink, Lidstrom said it wasn't his idea.

"I mostly drink beer," he said.

"What kind?"

"Any beer, really."

News alert: Lidstrom drinks beer!

Lidstrom was so swell that he suffered from a strange double standard. At a time when people criticized professional athletes for being too bold and too brash, people criticized him for being too bland and too boring. Some said his quiet style—on and off the ice—was the reason he had finished second for the Norris three years in a row before finally becoming the first European to win it—and the first to win it three years in a row since Boston's great Bobby Orr. *If only Nick were flashier, a better quote, the reporters who vote would've noticed him more, and maybe . . .*

Because Lidstrom wouldn't draw attention to himself, Yzerman often acted as his promoter.

"He's as good a defenseman as there has been in the league since I've been here," Yzerman said. "I watch him every day and really appreciate the little things he does. The majority of people don't notice those things."

Lidstrom had offensive skills that made him one of the top-scoring defensemen every season. He played pretty much perfect positional hockey on the defensive end. He picked passes out of the air with his stick, knocked down pucks with his feet, held off opposing forwards with what seemed like no effort, avoided checks, and still found ways to make tape-to-tape passes.

"If you get a chance—I always tell my friends this when they ask about the team—watch him closely," Yzerman said. "He's so good. He's so talented. He's head-and-shoulders above everybody."

So Lidstrom wasn't loud. So he didn't crash and bang, taking so few penalties that he was a four-time runner-up for the Lady Byng Memorial Trophy, awarded for sportsmanship, gentlemanly conduct, and a high standard of playing ability. That didn't mean he wasn't tough. He was as durable as anyone. He played so well through injuries—a pulled groin here, a broken nose there—that few outside the organization even knew it when he did. He had never played fewer than 78 games in a full season, and he had played almost 30 minutes per game most of his career. That meant he had been on the ice for the Wings almost half the time since 1991–1992, his rookie season.

"His leadership is going out and being the best player on the ice," Yzerman said. "He can go into a tough building against a physical team and still play his game, not shying away a bit. He can totally be counted on. That's what leadership is."

Nicklas Lidstrom Statistics

	Regular Season				Playoffs			
	GP	G	A	Pts.	GP	G	A	Pts.
1991–1992	80	11	49	60	11	1	2	3
1992–1993	84	7	34	41	7	1	0	1
1993–1994	84	10	46	56	7	3	2	5
1995	43	10	16	26	18	4	12	16
1995–1996	81	17	50	67	19	5	9	14
1996–1997	79	15	42	57	20	2	6	8
1997–1998	80	17	42	59	22	6	13	19
1998–1999	81	14	43	57	10	2	9	11
1999–2000	81	20	53	73	9	2	4	6
2000–2001	82	15	56	71	6	1	7	8
2001–2002	78	9	50	59	23	5	11	16
2002–2003	82	18	44	62	4	0	2	2
2003–2004	81	10	28	38	12	2	5	7
2005–2006	80	16	64	80	6	1	1	2
Totals	1,096	189	617	806	174	35	83	118

Stanley Cup: 1997, 1998, 2002

NHL All-Rookie Team: 1992

NHL First All-Star Team: 1998, 1999, 2000, 2001, 2002, 2003

Norris Trophy: 2001, 2002, 2003, 2006

Conn Smythe Trophy: 2002

NHL All-Star Game: 1996, 1998, 1999, 2000, 2001, 2002, 2003, 2004

Goaltender: Terry Sawchuk

Sawchuk's was a life of triumph and tragedy. He might have been the greatest goaltender in hockey history, but he only became a goaltender because as a 10-year-old he inherited the pads of his 17-year-old brother Mike, who died of a heart attack.

His rise to stardom was rapid. He was the rookie of the year in the United States Hockey League in 1947–1948 and in the American Hockey League in 1948–1949. He joined the Wings and won the Calder Memorial Trophy as the NHL's rookie of the year in 1950–1951. No one had done that before.

Adams took a risk trading Harry Lumley to Chicago to make room for Sawchuk. After all, Lumley was in net for the 1950 championship. He was a future Hall of Famer. But Adams was right to do it. People were calling Sawchuk the best of all time by his second season.

"There simply isn't any question about it," New York Rangers general manager Frank Boucher said in January 1952. "Oh, I know what some of the old-timers are going to say: 'That Sawchuk is just a kid and has to stand the test of time.' . . . But I'm sure that they'll be saying the same thing about Sawchuk years from now."

Sawchuk's goals-against average stayed below 2.00 his first five full seasons. He won the Vezina Trophy as the league's top goaltender in 1952, 1953, and 1955. He won the Cup in 1952, 1954, and 1955—allowing only five goals during the first run, none of them at home, as the Wings swept through the playoffs in eight games.

His style was innovative. At a time when goaltenders stood upright, Sawchuk crouched down. It allowed him to see the puck better through the forest of sticks and legs, and it allowed him to react more quickly to make saves. Soon other goaltenders started copying him.

But all was not well. Sawchuk had a handicap—one arm shorter than the other thanks to an injury suffered in a childhood football game—and endured all sorts of health problems. To go with all the hockey-related stuff—stitches and bruises, a bad back, and so on—his appendix ruptured one off-season and a lung collapsed in a car accident in another.

This is a man who lived hard and was famously moody, snapping at reporters, fans, just about everyone—even teammates. Defenseman Marcel Pronovost, his roommate on the road for years, was famous for saying he would say good morning to Sawchuk in French and English. "If he answered, I knew we would talk at least a little that day," he said. "But if he didn't reply, which was most days, we didn't speak the entire day."

Adams traded Sawchuk to the Boston Bruins in 1955. He had shipped out Lumley after the 1950 Cup to make room for Sawchuk; now he was doing the same thing to Sawchuk to make room for Glenn Hall. Adams brought back Sawchuk in 1957, and the Uke (as friends called Sawchuk because of his Ukrainian heritage) played the next seven seasons in Detroit.

After that, he bounced around. Three seasons with the Toronto Maple Leafs, including a Cup and a share of another Vezina. One season with the Los Angeles Kings. Another season with the Wings. Then one last campaign with the New York Rangers. Then one last tragedy.

Sawchuk shared a rental house on Long Island with Rangers teammate Ron Stewart. They got into a drunken, domestic argument over clean-up duties and household expenses and fought in their front yard. Sawchuk suffered stomach injuries that led to his death May 31, 1970.

A grand jury ruled Sawchuk's death was "completely accidental," clearing Stewart of wrongdoing. The Hockey Hall of Fame waived its waiting period to induct Sawchuk early.

Terry Sawchuk Statistics

	Regular Season						Playoffs				
	GP	W	L	T	SO	GAA	GP	W	L	SO	GAA
1949–1950	7	4	3	0	1	2.29	–	–	–	–	–
1950–1951	70	44	13	13	11	1.99	6	2	4	1	1.68
1951–1952	70	44	14	12	12	1.90	8	8	0	4	0.63
1952–1953	63	32	15	16	9	1.90	6	2	4	1	3.39
1953–1954	67	35	19	13	12	1.93	12	8	4	2	1.60
1954–1955	68	40	17	11	12	1.94	11	8	3	1	2.36
1957–1958	70	29	29	12	3	2.96	4	0	4	0	4.52
1958–1959	67	23	36	8	5	3.12	–	–	–	–	–
1959–1960	58	24	20	14	5	2.69	6	2	4	0	2.96
1960–1961	37	12	16	8	2	3.17	8	5	3	1	2.32
1961–1962	43	14	21	8	5	3.33	–	–	–	–	–
1962–1963	48	22	16	7	3	2.57	11	5	6	0	3.27
1963–1964	53	25	20	7	5	2.64	13	6	5	1	2.75
1968–1969	13	3	4	3	0	2.62	–	–	–	–	–
Totals	734	352	244	130	85	2.46	85	46	37	11	2.51

Stanley Cup: 1950, 1952, 1954, 1955

NHL First All-Star Team: 1951, 1952, 1953

Calder Memorial Trophy: 1951

Vezina Trophy: 1952, 1953, 1955

NHL Second All-Star Team: 1954, 1955, 1959, 1963

NHL All-Star Game: 1950, 1951, 1952, 1953, 1954, 1955, 1959, 1963, 1964

Hall of Fame

Coach and General Manager: Jack Adams

No one—not Gordie Howe, not Steve Yzerman—had a greater impact on the franchise than Jack Adams.

Of course, the word *impact* can be used positively and negatively.

Adams arrived as general manager and coach in 1927 when the team was called the Cougars. He gave up the coaching reins in 1946 but remained the GM until 1962. On his watch, the franchise went from receivership to championships. The Wings won seven Cups total, three while he was coach. The NHL named its Coach of the Year award for him. For a while, it had a division named for him, too.

A keen eye and an iron fist: those were Adams's assets. He was smart enough to sign the likes of Gordie Howe, Ted Lindsay, and Terry Sawchuk, and he was smart enough to extend the Wings' minor-league network throughout all of North America to give the organization incredible depth. He was demanding enough to push his players' talent to the limit. He hung a sign over the dressing room door that read, "We Supply Everything but the Guts."

Adams could be kind, like when he flew Howe's mother from Saskatchewan to Detroit when Howe suffered a serious head injury. He helped promote the game, going door-to-door to sell tickets during the Depression and writing an educational newspaper column called Follow the Puck.

But Adams was known for being callous. He'd throw oranges at his players. He'd threaten them with one-way tickets to the minors. Cross him, and he'd ship you out—no matter who you were. Just ask Hall of Famers Ted Lindsay and Red Kelly.

"When I played in Detroit, there was no dissension among players," Carl Liscombe, a Wing from 1937 to 1946, said in Paul Harris's *Heroes of Hockeytown from A to Z*. "We all hated Jack Adams."

Some say Adams cost the Wings as many Cups as he won them.

In 1942 the Wings had a 3–0 lead in the Finals over the Toronto Maple Leafs, but they blew it and lost in seven games—in large part because Adams went after an official after Game 4 and got suspended for the rest of the series.

Then, in 1955, the Wings had won four Cups in six years, and Adams proceeded to trade away half the team. Not for 42 years did the Wings win another Cup. Adams had stood pat after the back-to-back Cups of

1936 and 1937 and watched his team slip. He was determined not to let that happen again. But he went overboard.

"It was pathetic how Adams destroyed that team," Lindsay said in Richard Bak's *Detroit Red Wings: The Illustrated History*. "Of course, there was an uproar about it. But Adams generally was respected for what he had done for the Wings in other years. And then, he thought he was God anyway and could do no wrong."

Jack Adams's Coaching Record

	Regular Season				Playoffs			
	GC	W	L	T	GC	W	L	T
1927–1928	44	19	19	6	–	–	–	–
1928–1929	44	19	16	9	2	0	2	0
1929–1930	44	14	24	6	–	–	–	–
1930–1931	44	16	21	7	–	–	–	–
1931–1932	48	18	20	10	2	0	1	1
1932–1933	48	25	15	8	4	2	2	0
1933–1934	48	24	14	10	9	4	5	0
1934–1935	48	19	22	7	–	–	–	–
1935–1936	48	24	16	8	7	6	1	0
1936–1937	48	25	14	9	10	6	4	0
1937–1938	48	12	25	11	–	–	–	–
1938–1939	48	18	24	6	6	3	3	0
1939–1940	48	16	26	6	5	2	3	0
1940–1941	48	21	16	11	9	4	5	0
1941–1942	48	19	25	4	12	7	5	0
1942–1943	50	25	14	11	10	8	2	0
1943–1944	50	26	18	6	5	1	4	0
1944–1945	50	31	14	5	14	7	7	0
1945–1946	50	20	20	10	5	1	4	0
1946–1947	60	22	27	11	5	1	4	0
Totals	964	413	390	161	105	52	52	1

Stanley Cup: 1936, 1937, 1943

NHL First All-Star Team: 1937, 1943

NHL Second All-Star Team: 1945

Hall of Fame

Second Team
Forward: Sid Abel

The Production Line wouldn't have been so productive without Sid Abel. Young wingers Gordie Howe and Ted Lindsay learned a lot from the veteran center. The first season the three played together, 1948–1949, Abel won the Hart Memorial Trophy as the NHL's most valuable player.

Abel—known as "Bootnose" because of the way he looked after taking a punch from the Montreal Canadiens' Maurice Richard—played 12 seasons with the Wings, captaining the 1943 Stanley Cup team and helping lead the 1950 and 1952 teams to the Cup. You have to wonder how much more he—and the team—would have accomplished had he not missed the 1943–1944 and 1944–1945 seasons to serve in the Royal Canadian Air Force.

"Sid Abel, he was a great captain," forward Marty Pavelich said in Rich Kincaide's *The Gods of Olympia Stadium: Legends of the Detroit Red Wings.* "I sat beside him for quite a few years, because we went by our numbers. He was 12, and I was 11. He was just a great leader."

Abel made some forays out of the Motor City. He was player/coach of the Chicago Black Hawks. He was coach and general manager of the St. Louis Blues and GM of the Kansas City Scouts. But he kept coming back to Detroit. All told, he was a fixture for almost half a century.

He served the Wings as coach, general manager, and broadcaster, all in his calm, confident manner. Only Jack Adams (413) and Scotty Bowman (410) won more games as the Wings' coach than Abel (340) did.

"With Sid, you never played under pressure, even though it was there," forward Johnny Wilson said in Paul Harris's *Heroes of Hockeytown from A to Z.* "He made you feel like, 'Hey, you know, this is just another game. A back-alley game. Let's go have some fun.' . . . It took a lot of pressure off."

Sid Abel Statistics

	Regular Season				Playoffs			
	GP	G	A	Pts.	GP	G	A	Pts.
1938–1939	15	1	1	2	6	1	1	2
1939–1940	24	1	5	6	5	0	3	3
1940–1941	47	11	22	33	9	2	2	4
1941–1942	48	18	31	49	12	4	2	6
1942–1943	49	18	24	42	10	5	8	13

1945–1946	7	0	2	2	3	0	0	0
1946–1947	60	19	29	48	3	1	1	2
1947–1948	60	14	30	44	10	0	3	3
1948–1949	60	28	26	54	11	3	3	6
1949–1950	69	34	35	69	14	6	2	8
1950–1951	69	23	38	61	6	4	3	7
1951–1952	62	17	36	53	7	2	2	4
Totals	571	184	279	463	96	28	30	58

Stanley Cup: 1943, 1950, 1952

NHL First All-Star Team: 1949, 1950

NHL Second All-Star Team: 1942, 1951

Hart Trophy: 1949

NHL All-Star Game: 1949, 1950, 1951

Hall of Fame

Forward: Alex Delvecchio

Delvecchio was a constant in Detroit for almost a quarter of a century, and that doesn't even include his time as the Wings' coach and general manager.

He played 24 seasons for the Wings, from one game in 1950–1951, to 22 full seasons from 1951–1952 through 1972–1973, to 11 games in 1973–1974. Only Gordie Howe played more (25). Delvecchio played 1,549 games for the Wings. Only Howe played more (1,687). Delvecchio served 12 season as the Wings' captain, from the 1962–1963 season through his retirement. Only Steve Yzerman has served more (18 through 2003–2004).

Fats (as Delvecchio was known because of his round face) didn't put up fat numbers. He reached the 30-goal mark only once (31 in 1965–1966), and he reached the 80-point plateau only once (83 in 1968–1969). But he was remarkably consistent, and his 456 goals and 1,281 points rank behind only Howe and Yzerman in franchise history. He is perhaps known best for replacing Abel as the center on the Production Line between Howe and left wing Ted Lindsay.

With a smooth, seemingly effortless stride and a classy manner, Delvecchio won the Lady Byng Memorial Trophy for sportsmanship, gentlemanly conduct, and a high standard of playing ability three times, in 1958–1959, 1965–1966, and 1968–1969.

His style might have made him underappreciated by some, overshadowed by the likes of the Montreal Canadiens' Jean Beliveau and Henri Richard and the Chicago Black Hawks' Stan Mikita. But those who watched him game in and game out knew how good he really was.

"He wasn't like . . . some of those guys who could bust down the ice," said Johnny Wilson, who played with Delvecchio and coached him, in Paul Harris's book *Heroes of Hockeytown from A to Z*. "He methodically got down there and knew what the hell he was doing. Never got himself in a bind. Always knew where to move the puck. He kept the puck going."

Early in the Wings' 2001–2002 Stanley Cup season, as the Detroit Lions stumbled to a 35–0 loss to the St. Louis Rams and an 0–3 record that would become 0–12, the desperate, disappointed Silverdome crowd started chanting, "Let's go, Red Wings!" *Monday Night Football* funnyman Dennis Miller cracked that the fans wanted Alex Delvecchio at quarterback. Hey, with his passing skills, he might have helped.

Alex Delvecchio Statistics

	Regular Season				Playoffs			
	GP	G	A	Pts.	GP	G	A	Pts.
1950–1951	1	0	0	0	–	–	–	–
1951–1952	65	15	22	37	8	0	3	3
1952–1953	70	16	43	59	6	2	4	6
1953–1954	69	11	18	29	12	2	7	9
1954–1955	69	17	31	48	11	7	8	15
1955–1956	70	25	26	51	10	7	3	10
1956–1957	48	16	25	41	5	3	2	5
1957–1958	70	21	38	59	4	0	1	1
1958–1959	70	19	35	54	–	–	–	–
1959–1960	70	19	28	47	6	2	6	8
1960–1961	70	27	35	62	11	4	5	9
1961–1962	70	26	43	69	–	–	–	–
1962–1963	70	20	44	64	11	3	6	9
1963–1964	70	23	30	53	14	3	8	11
1964–1965	68	25	42	67	7	2	3	5
1965–1966	70	31	38	69	12	0	11	11

1966–1967	70	17	38	55	–	–	–	–
1967–1968	74	22	48	70	–	–	–	–
1968–1969	72	25	58	83	–	–	–	–
1969–1970	73	21	47	68	4	0	2	2
1970–1971	77	21	34	55	–	–	–	–
1971–1972	75	20	45	65	–	–	–	–
1972–1973	77	18	53	71	–	–	–	–
1973–1974	11	1	4	5	–	–	–	–
Totals	1,549	456	825	1,281	121	35	69	104

Stanley Cup: 1952, 1954, 1955

NHL Second All-Star Team: 1953, 1959

Lady Byng Memorial Trophy: 1959, 1966, 1969

NHL All-Star Game: 1953, 1954, 1955, 1956, 1957, 1958, 1959, 1961, 1962, 1963, 1964, 1965, 1967

Hall of Fame

Forward: Sergei Fedorov

Fedorov was the Wings' resident rock star from 1990–1991 to 2002–2003. Of course, he had the money: millions upon millions. But he also had the look: high cheekbones, flowing blond hair, flashy clothes. He had the charm: big smile, teenager's playfulness, trouble with English that made him misunderstood, a little mysterious, endearing. He had the talent: speedy skating, smooth stick handling, rocket shot. He had the girl: tennis sex symbol Anna Kournikova. Oh, and he had the drama.

After the Wings won the 1997 Cup, Kournikova waited for Fedorov in the dressing room, and she rode with him in the victory parade. When his teammates took the Cup on its first trip to Russia, he didn't go with them, and they criticized him for it. His contract expired, he and the Wings couldn't work out a deal, and he held out. People thought he was greedy; he wondered why the Wings didn't want him anymore.

"I took it pretty hard," he told the *Detroit Free Press*. "It was an ocean of emotions."

In public, he said he would never play for the Wings again. In private, he wondered if he could play for anyone else. Detroit was his second hometown. He held out until the 1998 Nagano Olympics, when he signed a six-year, $38 million offer sheet with the Carolina Hurricanes. The Wings matched it so they could keep him, he came back, and they won another Cup.

"Some people got mad because of what happened," he told the *Free Press*. "My challenge was to win some fans back."

Kournikova captured much of the fans' attention, not to mention the media's. Fedorov and Kournikova got engaged when she turned 18 in the summer of 1999. They didn't announce it, but that didn't matter. When she wasn't on tour, she was often seen in Detroit, at practices, at games. He endured snide comments and jokes about everything from her age to her looks to her athletic performance.

While the Kournikova comments never stopped—*Are they married? Did they break up? Is she with Enrique Iglesias now?*—neither did the comments about his play. He had a heart: he gave millions to charities. But some said he had no heart, in the hockey sense. He often didn't perform well if he didn't feel tip-top physically. Perhaps the worst thing he ever did was dominate the 1993–1994 season, scoring 56 goals and putting up 120 points, winning the Hart Memorial Trophy as the NHL's most valuable player, the Lester B. Pearson Award as the NHL Players' Association's most outstanding player, and the Selke Trophy as the league's best defensive forward. Although he was a great player afterward, winning the Selke once more in 1996, he didn't have the Hart, and so no one was satisfied. Fedorov eventually left for the Mighty Ducks of Anaheim as a free agent in 2003.

The bottom line, though, is this: in franchise history, Fedorov ranks fourth in regular-season scoring with 954 points and second in playoff scoring—behind Steve Yzerman and ahead of Gordie Howe—with 163 points. Ebbie Goodfellow, Sid Abel, and Howe are the only other Wings who have won the Hart.

Sergei Fedorov Statistics

	Regular Season				Playoffs			
	GP	G	A	Pts.	GP	G	A	Pts.
1990–1991	77	31	48	79	7	1	5	6
1991–1992	80	32	54	86	11	5	5	10
1992–1993	73	34	53	87	7	3	6	9
1993–1994	82	56	64	120	7	1	7	8
1995	42	20	30	50	17	7	17	24

1995–1996	78	39	68	107	19	2	18	20
1996–1997	74	30	33	63	20	8	12	20
1997–1998	21	6	11	17	22	10	10	20
1998–1999	77	26	37	63	10	1	8	9
1999–2000	68	27	35	62	9	4	4	8
2000–2001	75	32	37	69	6	2	5	7
2001–2002	81	31	37	68	23	5	14	19
2002–2003	80	36	47	83	4	1	2	3
Totals	908	400	554	954	162	50	113	163

Stanley Cup: 1997, 1998, 2002

NHL All-Rookie Team: 1991

NHL First All-Star Team: 1994

Selke Trophy: 1994, 1996

Pearson Award: 1994

Hart Memorial Trophy: 1994

NHL All-Star Game: 1992, 1994, 1996, 2001, 2002, 2003

Defense: Ebbie Goodfellow

Goodfellow was a Cougar, a Falcon, and a Red Wing. He started out as a center—and was a good one. In 1930–1931 and 1931–1932, the two years the franchise was known as the Falcons, he led the team in scoring. The first time, his 48 points ranked second in the NHL to the Montreal Canadiens' legendary Howie Morenz.

But because the Wings were well stocked up front with the likes of Larry Aurie, Marty Barry, and Herbie Lewis, general manager and coach Jack Adams asked Goodfellow to move to defense. And Goodfellow, being a good fellow, put the team ahead of himself by sacrificing his statistics. He went back to the blue line, and the move worked out well for the Wings and for him.

Goodfellow had the size and athletic ability to make the switch. He was 6', 180 pounds, and he was an excellent golfer, the caddie master at suburban Detroit's prestigious Oakland Hills. The Wings won back-to-back Stanley Cups in 1936 and 1937, and Goodfellow, at age 33, became the first Detroit player to win the Hart Memorial Trophy as the NHL's most valuable player in 1939–1940.

Not only did Goodfellow serve as captain of the Wings at different points, but he also served as a player/coach. He finished up with the Wings when they won the 1943 Cup and went on to coach the Chicago Black Hawks from 1950 to 1952.

Ebbie Goodfellow's Cougars, Falcons, Red Wings Statistics

	Regular Season				Playoffs			
	GP	G	A	Pts.	GP	G	A	Pts.
1929–1930 (Cougars)	44	17	17	34	–	–	–	–
1930–1931 (Falcons)	44	25	23	48	–	–	–	–
1931–1932	48	14	16	30	2	0	0	0
1932–1933 (Red Wings)	41	12	8	20	4	1	0	1
1933–1934	48	13	13	26	9	4	3	7
1934–1935	48	12	24	36	–	–	–	–
1935–1936	48	5	18	23	7	1	0	1
1936–1937	48	9	16	25	9	2	2	4
1937–1938	30	0	7	7	–	–	–	–
1938–1939	48	8	8	16	6	0	0	0
1939–1940	43	11	17	28	5	0	2	2
1940–1941	47	5	17	22	3	0	1	1
1941–1942	9	2	2	4	–	–	–	–
1942–1943	11	1	4	5	–	–	–	–
Totals	557	134	190	324	45	8	8	16

Stanley Cup: 1936, 1937, 1943

NHL Second All-Star Team: 1936

NHL First All-Star Team: 1937, 1940

Hart Memorial Trophy: 1940

NHL All-Star Game: 1937, 1939

Hall of Fame

Defense: Marcel Pronovost

When Gordie Howe suffered a severe head injury in the 1950 playoff opener, the Red Wings moved Red Kelly from defense to forward and called up

Pronovost from the Omaha Knights of the United States Hockey League. Pronovost was not yet 20. He had never played an NHL game. But he jumped onto the blue line and helped the Wings win the Stanley Cup.

Pronovost helped the Wings win the 1952, 1954, and 1955 Cups, too. Although not as well-known as Howe, Ted Lindsay, Terry Sawchuk, or Red Kelly, he was a big part of the dynasty. He had the ability to rush the puck well, but he didn't show it as much as he could have because the Wings already had an offensive wizard on defense in Kelly. He had the ability to hit hard—and he did show that.

"Man, would he rock 'em," forward Johnny Wilson said in Paul Harris's *Heroes of Hockeytown from A to Z*. "If he hit a guy head on, that guy was gone. He had some good ones. I saw him put some guys out of commission."

This is how respected Pronovost was: before a game March 5, 1960, the fans presented Pronovost with a new car—and these were Montreal Canadiens fans at the Forum. His Red Wings teammates gave him a diamond ring.

This is how tough Pronovost was: in the 1961 Stanley Cup Finals against the Chicago Black Hawks, Pronovost played on a broken ankle—coming to the rink on crutches, taking off his cast, and putting on his skates.

"I gave the game everything I had," Pronovost said in *Sports Illustrated*. "I wasn't afraid of anything.... Making a dangerous play on the ice didn't make me any more nervous than crossing the street might make someone else."

Pronovost played with the Wings until they traded him to the Toronto Maple Leafs in 1965. He won another Cup in Toronto, then stayed in hockey in different capacities in different leagues, including a nine-game stint as the Wings' coach in 1979–1980.

Marcel Pronovost Statistics

	Regular Season				Playoffs			
	GP	G	A	Pts.	GP	G	A	Pts.
1949–1950	–	–	–	–	9	0	1	1
1950–1951	37	1	6	7	6	0	0	0
1951–1952	69	7	11	18	8	0	1	1
1952–1953	68	8	19	27	6	0	0	0
1953–1954	57	6	12	18	12	2	3	5

	Regular Season				Playoffs			
	GP	G	A	Pts.	GP	G	A	Pts.
1954–1955	70	9	25	34	11	1	2	3
1955–1956	68	4	13	17	10	0	2	2
1956–1957	70	7	9	16	5	0	0	0
1957–1958	62	2	18	20	4	0	1	1
1958–1959	69	11	21	32	–	–	–	–
1959–1960	69	7	17	24	6	1	1	2
1960–1961	70	6	11	17	9	2	3	5
1961–1962	70	4	14	18	–	–	–	–
1962–1963	69	4	9	13	11	1	4	5
1963–1964	67	3	17	20	14	0	2	2
1964–1965	68	1	15	16	7	0	3	3
Totals	983	80	217	297	118	7	23	30

Stanley Cup: 1950, 1952, 1954, 1955

NHL Second All-Star Team: 1958, 1959

NHL First All-Star Team: 1960, 1961

NHL All-Star Game: 1950, 1954, 1955, 1957, 1958, 1959, 1960, 1961, 1963, 1965

Hall of Fame

Goaltender: Chris Osgood

Osgood might seem like an odd choice for a Wings all-time team. When he played in Detroit from 1993–1994 to 2000–2001, he was often viewed as a weakness, not a strength.

With only 41 games of NHL experience, Osgood found himself in the net in the first round of the 1994 playoffs, after starter Bob Essensa lost twice to the San Jose Sharks. In Game 7, Osgood strayed from the net, played the puck—and sent it straight to San Jose forward Jaime Baker, who scored the winner with 6:35 left. In the dressing room afterward, he sobbed and kept repeating, "I'm so sorry," and some people never got over that.

Osgood played most of the 1996–1997 season, but Scotty Bowman went with veteran Mike Vernon in the playoffs, and Vernon won the Conn Smythe Trophy as the playoffs' most valuable player when the Wings won the Cup. The Wings won the 1998 Cup with Osgood in goal, but many remembered only the 90-footers he allowed to the St. Louis Blues in the second round and to the Dallas Stars in the third. They said the Wings won the Cup not because of him but in spite of him.

"There has been the perception out there that when the Red Wings win, we win because of our skaters," Ken Holland said, "and when we lose, we lose because of our goaltending."

When Holland acquired Dominik Hasek to replace Osgood in 2001, he had trouble trading Osgood because of Osgood's large contract. Osgood ended up going to the New York Islanders via the waiver draft. He was later traded to the St. Louis Blues.

Because of all that, it's easy to forget a few things. Statistically, Osgood ranks second only to Terry Sawchuk among Detroit Red Wings goaltenders—second in games (389), second in wins (221), second in shutouts (30). He was 28 when he left Detroit with those numbers. At 28, Patrick Roy, the NHL's all-time wins leader, had 225 wins in 418 games and 20 shutouts. Sawchuk was in net for three Wings Cups. Osgood was in net for one, tying for second with six others—Normie Smith, Earl Robertson, Johnny Mowers, Harry Lumley, Vernon, and Hasek.

Sure, Osgood played for a great Detroit team. But so did those other netminders. No, he didn't win a Vezina Trophy as the league's best goaltender with the Wings as Smith, Mowers, and Sawchuk did. And no, he probably won't be joining Lumley, Sawchuk, Glenn Hall, and Hasek in the Hall of Fame. But after Sawchuk, he did more in a Wings uniform than any other goaltender. He must have been doing something right.

Said center Kris Draper, one of Osgood's best friends, "I don't think he's gotten the credit he deserves."

Chris Osgood Statistics

	Regular Season						Playoffs				
	GP	W	L	T	SO	GAA	GP	W	L	SO	GAA
1993–1994	41	23	8	5	2	2.86	6	3	2	1	2.35
1995	19	14	5	0	1	2.26	2	0	0	0	1.76
1995–1996	50	39	6	5	5	2.17	15	8	7	2	2.12
1996–1997	47	23	13	9	6	2.30	2	0	0	0	2.55
1997–1998	64	33	20	11	6	2.21	22	16	6	2	2.12
1998–1999	63	34	25	4	3	2.42	6	4	2	1	2.35

	Regular Season						Playoffs				
	GP	W	L	T	SO	GAA	GP	W	L	SO	GAA
1999–2000	53	30	14	8	6	2.40	9	5	4	2	1.97
2000–2001	52	25	19	4	1	2.69	6	2	4	1	2.47
Totals	389	221	110	46	30	2.40	68	38	25	9	2.16

Stanley Cup: 1997, 1998

NHL Second All-Star Team: 1996

Shared Jennings Trophy with Mike Vernon: 1996

NHL All-Star Game: 1996, 1997, 1998

Coach: Scotty Bowman

Bowman was the greatest coach in hockey history—maybe in professional sports history. He won a record nine Stanley Cups as a coach during an incomparable NHL career that stretched from the 1960s to the 2000s, and he spent more time in Detroit—nine seasons—than he spent anywhere else.

There is only one reason Bowman places second to Jack Adams here. Adams spent so long with the Wings he was synonymous with them; Bowman probably will be remembered more as a Montreal Canadien because he led the Habs to four straight Cups in the seventies.

During his stint in Detroit, Bowman added to his legend as a one-of-a-kind winner.

He was old-fashioned, but he knew how and when to change. He continued to be an innovator. When the Wings had five talented Russians in the nineties, he put them on one unit—dubbed the "Russian Five"—to take advantage of their native puck-possession style in a North American, dump-and-chase league. As Brendan Shanahan once pointed out, "He started coaching guys who had summer jobs and crew cuts, and now he's coaching guys with Ferraris, earrings, blond streaks, and agents."

"The thing is, Scotty's methods have stood the test of time," said Ken Hitchcock, who coached against Bowman in later years. "Most people that are in his status, the Woody Hayeses, the Bobby Knights, the elite coaches that have won on a consistent basis with old-school techniques, have not adjusted to new-school personalities. Scotty's kept the same ideas and the same principles, but he's adjusted with the times."

All he wanted to do was win.

The *Detroit Free Press* told this story: Bowman asked the woman who became his wife to attend games when he was starting out with St. Louis in the late sixties. But there was a catch: if the Blues won, she would wait for him outside the dressing room. If they lost, she should go home, because he wouldn't be in the best of moods.

"The Blues were in the middle of a long losing streak, so I never got to see him," Suella Bowman said. "Then they tied a game, and me not knowing much about the game, I thought that was a pretty good thing, because at least it wasn't a loss. So I waited for Scott."

She waited. And waited. After about two hours, she finally asked a dressing-room attendant if he was still around.

"And then, all of a sudden, he comes out and looks surprised that I was there, because they hadn't won," she said. "I found out then that there was no middle ground with Scott. If it's not a win, nothing else would be acceptable."

Scotty Bowman's Record

	Regular Season				Playoffs		
	GC	W	L	T	GC	W	L
1993–1994	84	46	30	8	7	3	4
1995	48	33	11	4	18	12	6
1995–1996	82	62	13	7	19	10	9
1996–1997	82	38	26	18	20	16	4
1997–1998	82	44	23	15	22	16	6
1998–1999	77	39	31	7	10	6	4
1999–2000	82	48	24	10	9	5	4
2000–2001	82	49	24	9	6	2	4
2001–2002	82	51	21	10	23	16	7
Totals	701	410	203	88	134	86	48

Jack Adams Award: 1996

Hall of Fame

General Manager: Jimmy Devellano

When Mike Ilitch bought the Red Wings from the Norris family in 1982, Devellano was the first person he hired. Devellano had helped build the New York Islanders into champions as a scout and assistant general manager. Now he had a tough task in front of him as the Wings' GM.

The franchise, as Devellano has said often, was in the Detroit River. There were 2,100 season-ticket holders. Not only was there no waiting list, there was no waiting for anything. Concessions? Bathroom? Step right up. The Wings had missed the playoffs for five straight years, 10 times in 12 years.

"It was not Hockeytown," Devellano said. "The fans had left the team. It was pretty apparent that we really now had to do something to sell tickets, had to somehow give the fans and the press something with a little more hope, something with a little more pizzazz."

Devellano was responsible for bringing in people from Steve Yzerman to Scotty Bowman. As the Wings worked on building a foundation through the draft—taking a risk that paid off in selecting Soviet players— they worked on rebuilding their relationship with the fans by acquiring big-name players and hiring big-name coaches. Slowly but surely the Wings improved until they enjoyed an era that rivaled the fifties in glory.

Although Devellano resigned as general manager in 1990, he remained in the front office and served as Ilitch's trusted advisor. He deserves a good deal of credit. In 2002, 20 years after Devellano's arrival, Joe Louis Arena was sold out all the time. There were about seventeen thousand season-ticket holders. There was a waiting list. The Wings had won three Stanley Cups in six years—and with an all-world cast that played with pizzazz.

Third Team

Forward: Larry Aurie

When general manager and coach Jack Adams took over the franchise in 1927, he signed Aurie. "Little Dempsey," as the 5'6", 145-pound Aurie was called, went on to spend his entire 11-year NHL career with the Cougars, Falcons, and Red Wings. He helped the Wings win back-to-back Stanley Cups in 1936 and 1937, scoring a league-leading 23 goals in the 1936–1937 season. His impact on the franchise as it rose from the ashes should not be forgotten.

Larry Aurie's Cougars, Falcons, Red Wings Statistics

	Regular Season				Playoffs			
	GP	G	A	Pts.	GP	G	A	Pts.
1927–1928	44	13	3	16	–	–	–	–
(Cougars)								
1928–1929	35	1	1	2	2	1	0	1
1929–1930	43	14	5	19	–	–	–	–
1930–1931	41	12	6	18	–	–	–	–
(Falcons)								
1931–1932	48	12	8	20	2	0	0	0
1932–1933	45	12	11	23	4	1	0	1
(Red Wings)								
1933–1934	48	16	19	35	9	3	7	10
1934–1935	48	17	29	46	–	–	–	–
1935–1936	44	16	18	34	7	1	2	3
1936–1937	45	23	20	43	–	–	–	–
1937–1938	47	10	9	19	–	–	–	–
1939–1940	1	1	0	1	–	–	–	–
Totals	489	147	129	276	24	6	9	15

Stanley Cup: 1936, 1937

NHL First All-Star Team: 1937

NHL All-Star Game: 1934

Forward: Syd Howe

Gordie Howe wasn't the only longtime Wing with the last name Howe who retired as the NHL's all-time leading scorer.

Syd Howe (no relation) came to Detroit from the St. Louis Eagles in 1935 and finished the season second in league scoring with 47 points. He helped the Wings win the Stanley Cup in 1936, 1937, and 1943. Howe could play defense, but mostly he played center or left wing.

When he retired in 1946, he had 528 points—237 goals, 291 assists—more than anyone else in league history.

Syd Howe Statistics

	Regular Season				Playoffs			
	GP	G	A	Pts.	GP	G	A	Pts.
1934–1935	14	8	12	20	–	–	–	–
1935–1936	48	16	14	30	7	3	3	6
1936–1937	45	17	10	27	10	2	5	7
1937–1938	48	8	19	27	–	–	–	–
1938–1939	48	16	20	36	6	3	1	4
1939–1940	46	14	23	37	5	2	2	4
1940–1941	48	20	24	44	9	1	7	8
1941–1942	48	16	19	35	12	3	5	8
1942–1943	50	20	35	55	7	1	2	3
1943–1944	46	32	28	60	5	2	2	4
1944–1945	46	17	36	53	7	0	0	0
1945–1946	26	4	7	11	–	–	–	–
Totals	513	188	247	435	68	17	27	44

Stanley Cup: 1936, 1937, 1943

NHL Second All-Star Team: 1945

NHL All-Star Game: 1939

Hall of Fame

Forward: Norm Ullman

Norm Ullman shunned the spotlight, and playing with the likes of Gordie Howe, he stayed in the shadows. But he was an excellent skater and stick handler, he was remarkably consistent and durable, and he put together an outstanding career. He produced 758 points as a Wing, ranking him fifth in team history. He was traded to the Toronto Maple Leafs in 1968 in the deal that brought Frank Mahovlich to Detroit.

Norm Ullman Statistics

	Regular Season				Playoffs			
	GP	G	A	Pts.	GP	G	A	Pts.
1955–1956	66	9	9	18	10	1	3	4
1956–1957	64	16	36	52	5	1	1	2
1957–1958	69	23	28	51	4	0	2	2
1958–1959	69	22	36	58	–	–	–	–

1959–1960	70	24	34	58	6	2	2	4
1960–1961	70	28	42	70	11	0	4	4
1961–1962	70	26	38	64	–	–	–	–
1962–1963	70	26	30	56	11	4	12	16
1963–1964	61	21	30	51	14	7	10	17
1964–1965	70	42	41	83	7	6	4	10
1965–1966	70	31	41	72	12	6	9	15
1966–1967	68	26	44	70	–	–	–	–
1967–1968	58	30	25	55	–	–	–	–
Totals	875	324	434	758	80	27	47	74

NHL First All-Star Team: 1965

NHL Second All-Star Team: 1967

NHL All-Star Game: 1955, 1960, 1961, 1962, 1963, 1964, 1965, 1967, 1968

Hall of Fame

Defense: "Black" Jack Stewart

Stewart was a swift skater who was good with the puck, but he was known for his toughness. He was most famous for a fight he had with the Chicago Black Hawks' John Mariucci—a bloody 15-minute affair that went from the ice to the penalty box. His career might have been even more remarkable had he not missed two NHL seasons to play military hockey during World War II. He was traded to Chicago with goaltender Harry Lumley in 1950 and played two more seasons, retiring in 1952.

Jack Stewart Statistics

	Regular Season				Playoffs			
	GP	G	A	Pts.	GP	G	A	Pts.
1938–1939	32	0	1	1	–	–	–	–
1939–1940	48	1	0	1	5	0	0	0
1940–1941	47	2	6	8	9	1	2	3
1941–1942	44	4	7	11	12	0	1	1
1942–1943	44	2	9	11	10	1	2	3
1945–1946	47	4	11	15	5	0	0	0
1946–1947	55	5	9	14	5	0	1	1
1947–1948	60	5	14	19	9	1	3	4

	Regular Season				Playoffs			
	GP	G	A	Pts.	GP	G	A	Pts.
1948–1949	60	4	11	15	11	1	1	2
1949–1950	65	3	11	14	14	1	4	5
Totals	502	30	79	109	80	5	14	19

Stanley Cup: 1943, 1950

NHL First-All Star Team: 1943, 1948, 1949

NHL Second All-Star Team: 1946, 1947

NHL All-Star Game: 1947, 1948, 1949, 1950

Hall of Fame

Defense: Reed Larson

The Wings weren't much good when Larson played for them, but he was good enough to surpass Red Kelly as the team's all-time leading scorer among defensemen. He held that distinction until Nicklas Lidstrom passed him years later. The Minnesota native also was the all-time leading scorer among American-born NHLers for a while. His 570 points as a Wing rank eighth in team history. Larson was traded to the Boston Bruins in 1986 and bounced around with four other teams afterward.

Reed Larson Statistics

	Regular Season				Playoffs			
	GP	G	A	Pts.	GP	G	A	Pts.
1976–1977	14	0	1	1	–	–	–	–
1977–1978	75	19	41	60	7	0	2	2
1978–1979	79	18	49	67	–	–	–	–
1979–1980	80	22	44	66	–	–	–	–
1980–1981	78	27	31	58	–	–	–	–
1981–1982	80	21	39	60	–	–	–	–
1982–1983	80	22	52	74	–	–	–	–
1983–1984	78	23	39	62	4	2	0	2
1984–1985	77	17	45	62	3	1	2	3
1985–1986	67	19	41	60	–	–	–	–
Totals	708	188	382	570	14	3	4	7

NHL All-Star Game: 1978, 1980, 1981

Goaltender: Harry Lumley

A few men could easily have been the Wings' third-team goaltender. Normie Smith and Johnny Mowers won the Vezina Trophy as the NHL's top goaltender while they were Wings. Mike Vernon won the Conn Smythe Trophy as the playoffs' most valuable player when he was a Wing. Dominik Hasek set the league record for playoff shutouts (six) as a Wing. All won the Stanley Cup in Detroit. But the nod goes to Lumley, even though he spent the best years of his career as a Toronto Maple Leaf. He was in goal when the Wings won the Cup in 1950, and he ranks third in team history in games (324), wins (163), and shutouts (26). He was traded to the Chicago Black Hawks after the 1950 Cup victory to make room for Terry Sawchuk.

Harry Lumley Statistics

	Regular Season						Playoffs				
	GP	W	L	T	SO	Avg.	GP	W	L	SO	Avg.
1943–1944	2	0	2	0	0	6.50	–	–	–	–	–
1944–1945	37	24	10	3	1	3.22	14	7	7	2	2.14
1945–1946	50	20	20	10	2	3.18	5	1	4	1	3.11
1946–1947	52	22	20	10	3	3.06	–	–	–	–	–
1947–1948	60	30	18	12	7	2.46	10	4	6	0	3.00
1948–1949	60	34	19	7	6	2.42	11	4	7	0	2.15
1949–1950	63	33	16	14	7	2.35	14	8	6	3	1.85
Totals	324	163	107	54	26	2.73	54	24	30	6	2.26

Stanley Cup: 1950

Hall of Fame

Coach: Tommy Ivan

Tommy Ivan coached Gordie Howe in the minor leagues. He spent six seasons as the Wings' head coach, and they finished in first place each time. They won the Stanley Cup under him in 1950, 1952, and 1954. He then left for the Chicago Black Hawks, leaving Jimmy Skinner to coach the Wings to the 1955 Cup, apparently because he clashed with general manager Jack Adams.

Tommy Ivan Record

	Regular Season				Playoffs		
	GC	W	L	T	GC	W	L
1947–1948	60	38	18	12	10	4	6
1948–1949	60	34	19	7	11	4	7
1949–1950	70	37	19	14	14	8	6
1950–1951	70	44	13	13	6	2	4
1951–1952	70	44	14	12	8	8	0
1952–1953	70	36	16	18	6	2	4
1953–1954	70	37	19	14	12	8	4
Totals	470	262	118	90	67	36	31

Stanley Cup: 1950, 1952, 1954

Hall of Fame

General Manager: Ken Holland

Ken Holland rose to general manager in 1997, when the Wings won the second of back-to-back Cups, so it's true that he inherited a great team. It's also true that he had the advantage of one of the biggest budgets in the NHL, thanks to owner Mike Ilitch. But Holland helped build the Wings of the late nineties as a scout and assistant GM, and when he got his hands on Ilitch's money, he spent it wisely. Many thought the Wings were washed up after their first-round loss to the Los Angeles Kings in 2001. But Holland acquired Dominik Hasek, Luc Robitaille, and Brett Hull that summer, giving the Wings nine potential Hall of Famers, and they finished a storybook season with another Cup in 2002.

ANSWERS TO TRIVIA QUESTIONS

Page 2: D.

Page 4: A. The Wings played their first season across the Detroit River in Windsor, Ontario. They moved into the Olympia in November 1927.

Page 6: B. But the game wasn't a tradition—played almost every year—until the forties.

Page 9: C. Mickey Redmond scored 52 in 1972–1973.

Page 15: C.

Page 21: D. Nicklas Lidstrom has been runner-up four times, but to the surprise of many, he has never won the Lady Byng.

Page 25: Lefty Wilson. Assistant trainers once served as backup goaltenders, and sometimes the home team's assistant trainer had to replace the road team's injured goaltender. Wilson came in for the Wings' Terry Sawchuk in 1953, the Leafs' Harry Lumley in 1956, and the Bruins' Don Simmons in 1957. In 81 minutes, Wilson allowed only one goal.

Page 28: C. Gordie Howe wore No. 17 from 1946–1947 to 1947–1948. He switched to No. 9 because players with lower numbers got better bunks on the team train.

Page 30: C. No. 7 is retired in honor of Ted Lindsay, who wore it from 1946–1947 to 1956–1957. But Lindsay wore No. 15 in 1964–1965, when he came back to Detroit after playing for Chicago from 1957–1958 to 1959–1960 and not playing from 1960–1961 to 1963–1964. Lindsay wore No. 14 from 1944–1945 to 1946–1947.

Page 41: True. The original Grind Line was Kirk Maltby, Kris Draper, and Joe Kocur. Later it became Maltby, Draper, and Darren McCarty.

Page 47: No. 6 for Larry Aurie, who starred for the franchise from 1927–1928 to 1938–1939, and No. 16 for Vladimir Konstantinov, who suffered career-ending injuries in a limousine accident six days after the Wings won the 1997 Stanley Cup.

Page 49: D. The Russian Five—the all-Russian unit used by coach Scotty Bowman in the nineties—were Sergei Fedorov, Slava Fetisov, Vladimir Konstantinov, Slava Kozlov, and Igor Larionov.

Page 55: All of the above. The Wings are 8–7–4 on Halloween, 30–21–9 on New Year's Eve, 16–13–5 on Valentine's Day, and 17–12–2 on St. Patrick's Day.

Page 58: C. Lee Norwood and Gilbert Delorme were known as Hack and Whack.

Page 62: B.

Page 67: Three. They took Claude Gauthier in 1964, Dale McCourt in 1977, and Joe Murphy in 1986.

Page 78: Technically, Jimmy Devellano, Red Wings senior vice president, hockey operations. No one held the title of GM from 1994–1995 to 1996–1997.

Page 95: B. Ted Lindsay led the league in scoring with 78 points in 1949–1950 with the Red Wings. He led the league in penalty minutes with 184 in 1958–1959 with Chicago.

Page 125: True. But not that Scotty Bowman. It was Ralph "Scotty" Bowman, no relation to the legend who would later coach the team.

Page 133: True. Gretzky produced more than 155 points in a season nine times and Lemieux did it four times.

Page 141: True. Pete Babando scored 28:31 into overtime in Game 7 of the 1950 Finals against the New York Rangers, and Tony Leswick scored 4:20 into overtime in Game 7 of the 1954 Finals against Montreal. No one else has won the Cup in Game 7 in OT.

Page 149: A. Syd Howe scored six goals in a 12–2 victory over the New York Rangers on February 3, 1944.

Detroit Red Wings All-Time Roster (through the 2005–2006 season)

Players on this roster have appeared in at least one game with the Red Wings.

A

Gerry Abel, LW	1966–1967
Sid Abel, C-LW	1938–1939 to 1942–1943, 1945–1946 to 1951–1952
Gene Achtymichuk, C	1958–1959
Greg Adams, LW	1989–1990
Micah Aivazoff, LW	1993–1994
Gary Aldcorn, LW	1959–1960 to 1960–1961
Keith Allen, D	1953–1954 to 1954–1955
Ralph Almas, G	1946–1947, 1952–1953
Dave Amadio, D	1957–1958
Dale Anderson, D	1956–1957
Earl Anderson, RW	1974–1975
Ron Anderson, RW	1967–1968 to 1968–1969
Tom Anderson, C	1934–1935
Al Arbour, D	1953–1954, 1955–1956 to 1957–1958
Jack Arbour, D-LW	1926–1927
Murray Armstrong, C	1943–1944 to 1945–1946
Brent Ashton, LW	1986–1987 to 1987–1988
Ossie Asmundson, RW	1934–1935
Pierre Aubry, C-LW	1983–1984 to 1984–1985
Phillipe Audet, LW	1998–1999
Larry Aurie, RW	1927–1928 to 1938–1939
Sean Avery, C	2001–2002

B

Pete Babando, LW	1949–1950
Bob Bailey, RW	1956–1957 to 1957–1958
Garnet "Ace" Bailey, LW	1972–1973 to 1973–1974
Doug Baldwin, D	1946–1947
Doug Barkley, D	1962–1963 to 1965–1966
Ryan Barnes, LW	2003–2004
Dave Barr, RW	1986–1987 to 1990–1991
John Barrett, D	1980–1981 to 1985–1986
Marty Barry, C	1935–1936 to 1938–1939
Hank Bassen, G	1960–1961 to 1963–1964, 1965–1966 to 1966–1967
Frank Bathe, D	1974–1975 to 1975–1976
Andy Bathgate, C-RW	1965–1966 to 1966–1967
Bob Baun, D	1968–1969 to 1970–1971
Sergei Bautin, D	1993–1994
Red Beattie, LW	1937–1938
Clarence Behling, D	1940–1941 to 1942–1943
Pete Bellefeuille, RW	1926–1927, 1928–1929 to 1929–1930
Frank Bennett, C	1943–1944
Red Berenson, C	1970–1971 to 1974–1975
Michel Bergeron, RW	1974–1975 to 1977–1978
Marc Bergevin, D	1995–1996
Gary Bergman, D	1964–1965 to 1974–1975
Thommie Bergman, D	1972–1973 to 1974–1975, 1977–1978 to 1979–1980
Fred Berry, C	1976–1977

Phil Besler, RW	1938–1939
Pete Bessone, D	1937–1938
Allan Bester, G	1990–1991 to 1991–1992
Bill Beveridge, G	1929–1930
Tim Bissett, C	1990–1991
Steve Black, LW	1949–1950 to 1950–1951
Tom Bladon, D	1980–1981
Mike Blaisdell, RW	1980–1981 to 1982–1983
Mike Bloom, LW	1974–1975 to 1976–1977
John Blum, D	1988–1989
Marc Boileau, C	1961–1962
Patrick Boileau, D	2002–2003
Gilles Boisvert, G	1959–1960
Leo Boivin, D	1965–1966 to 1966–1967
Ivan Boldirev, C-LW	1982–1983 to 1984–1985
Dan Bolduc, RW	1978–1979 to 1979–1980
Marcel Bonin, LW	1952–1953 to 1954–1955
Darryl Bootland, RW	2003–2004
Henry Boucha, LW	1971–1972 to 1973–1974
Claude Bourque, G	1939–1940
Ralph "Scotty" Bowman, D	1934–1935 to 1939–1940
Rick Bowness, RW	1977–1978
Yank Boyd, RW	1934–1935
John Brenneman, LW	1967–1968
Carl Brewer, D	1969–1970
Archie Briden, LW	1926–1927
Mel Bridgman, LW-C	1986–1987 to 1987–1988
Bernie Brophy, C	1928–1929 to 1929–1930
Adam Brown, LW	1941–1942 to 1943–1944, 1945–1946 to 1946–1947
Andy Brown, G	1971–1972 to 1972–1973
Arnie Brown, D	1970–1971 to 1971–1972
Connie Brown, C	1938–1939 to 1942–1943
Doug Brown, RW-LW	1995 to 2000–2001
Gerry Brown, LW	1941–1942, 1945–1946
Larry Brown, D	1970–1971
Stan Brown, D	1927–1928

Jeff Brubaker, C	1988–1989
Ed Bruneteau, RW	1941–1942, 1943–1944 to 1948–1949
Mud Bruneteau, RW	1935–1936 to 1945–1946
Bill Brydge, D	1928–1929
Johnny Bucyk, LW	1955–1956 to 1956–1957
Tony Bukovich, LW	1943–1944 to 1944–1945
Hy Buller, D	1943–1944 to 1944–1945
Charlie Burns, C	1958–1959
Shawn Burr, C	1984–1985 to 1995
Cummy Burton, LW	1955–1956, 1957–1958 to 1958–1959
Eddie Bush, D	1938–1939, 1941–1942
Walter Buswell, D	1932–1933 to 1934–1935
Yuri Butsayev, C	1999–2000 to 2000–2001
Dmiti Bykov, D	2002–2003

C

Al Cameron, D	1975–1976 to 1978–1979
Craig Cameron, RW	1966–1967
Colin Campbell, D	1982–1983 to 1984–1985
Terry Carkner, D	1993–1994 to 1995
Gene Carrigan, C	1932–1933 to 1933–1934
Billy Carroll, C	1985–1986 to 1986–1987
Greg Carroll, C	1978–1979
Dwight Carruthers, D	1965–1966
Frank Carson, RW	1931–1932 to 1933–1934
Jimmy Carson, C	1989–1990 to 1992–1993
Joe Carveth, RW-C	1940–1941 to 1945–1946, 1949–1950 to 1950–1951
Bart Cashley, D	1965–1966 to 1968–1969, 1974–1975
Frank Cernik, LW	1984–1985
John Chabot, C	1987–1988 to 1990–1991
Steve Chaisson, D	1987–1988 to 1993–1994
Milan Chalupa, D	1984–1985
Bob Champoux, G	1963–1964
Guy Charron, C-LW	1970–1971 to 1974–1975

Lude Check, LW	1943–1944	Ray Cullen, C	1966–1967
Chris Chelios, D	1998–1999 to 2003–2004,	Jim Cummins, LW	1991–1992 to 1992–1993
	2005–2006	Ian Cushenan, D	1963–1964
Tim Cheveldae, G	1988–1989 to 1993–1994		
Real Chevrefils, LW	1955–1956	**D**	
Alain Chevrier, G	1990–1991	Frank Daley, D-LW	1928–1929
Chris Chihocki, RW	1985–1986 to 1986–1987	Joe Daley, G	1971–1972
Dino Ciccarelli, RW	1992–1993 to 1995–1996	Mathieu Dandenault, RW-D	1995–1996
Wendel Clark, LW	1998–1999		to 2003–2004
Daniel Cleary, F	2005–2006	Pavel Datsyuk, C	2001–2002 to 2003–2004,
Rejean Cloutier, D	1979–1980 to 1981–1982		2005–2006
Roland Cloutier, D	1977–1978 to 1978–1979	Bob Davis, D	1932–1933
Steve Coates, RW	1976–1977	Lorne Davis, RW	1954–1955
Paul Coffey, D	1992–1993 to 1995–1996	Mal Davis, RW	1978–1979 to 1980–1981
Bill Collins, RW	1970–1971 to 1973–1974	Billy Dea, LW	1956–1957 to 1957–1958,
Brian Conacher, C	1971–1972		1969–1970 to 1970–1971
Charlie Conacher, RW	1938–1939	Don Deacon, C	1936–1937,
Jim Conacher, LW	1945–1946 to 1948–1949		1938–1939 to 1939–1940
Roy Conacher, LW	1946–1947	Nelson DeBenedet, LW	1973–1974
Alex Connell, G	1931–1932	Denis De Jordy, G	1972–1973 to 1973–1974
Wayne Connelly, RW	1968–1969 to 1970–1971	Gilbert Delorme, D	1987–1988 to 1988–1989
Bob Conners, C	1928–1929 to 1929–1930	Alex Delvecchio, C-LW	1950–1951 to 1973–1974
Bob Cook, RW	1972–1973	Boyd Devereaux, C	2000–2001 to 2003–2004
Carson Cooper, RW	1927–1928 to 1931–1932	Al Dewsbury, D	1946–1947 to 1947–1948,
Norm Corcoran, RW	1955–1956		1949–1950
Murray Costello, C	1955–1956 to 1956–1957	Ed Diachuk, LW	1960–1961
Gerry Couture, RW	1944–1945 to 1950–1951	Bob Dillabough, LW	1961–1962 to 1964–1965
Abbie Cox, G	1933–1934	Cecil Dilon, RW	1939–1940
Danny Cox, LW	1931–1932	Bill Dineen, RW	1953–1954 to 1957–1958
Murray Craven, LW-C	1982–1983 to 1983–1984	Peter Dineen, D	1989–1990
Bobby Crawford, C	1982–1983	Connie Dion, G	1943–1944 to 1944–1945
Jim Creighton, C	1930–1931 to 1931–1932	Marcel Dionne, C	1971–1972 to 1974–1975
Cory Cross, D	2005–2006	Per Djoos, D	1990–1991
Doug Crossman, D	1990–1991 to 1991–1992	Gary Doak, D	1965–1966, 1972–1973
Gary Croteau, LW	1969–1970	Bobby Dollas, D	1990–1991 to 1992–1993
Troy Crowder, RW	1991–1992	Dolly Dolson, G	1928–1929 to 1930–1931
Roger Crozier, G	1963–1964 to 1969–1970	Lloyd Doran, C	1946–1947
Wilf Cude, G	1933–1934	Red Doran, D	1937–1938
Barry Cullen, RW	1959–1960	Ken Doraty, RW	1937–1938

Kent Douglas, D	1967–1968 to 1968–1969
Les Douglas, C	1940–1941, 1942–1943, 1946–1947
Dallas Drake, C-LW	1992–1993 to 1993–1994
Kris Draper, C	1993–1994 to 2003–2004, 2005–2006
Rene Drolet, RW	1974–1975
Clarence Drouillard, C	1937–1938
Gilles Dube, LW	1953–1954
Steve Duchesne, D	1999–2000 to 2001–2002
Ron Duguay, RW-C	1983–1984 to 1985–1986
Lorne Duguid, LW	1934–1935 to 1935–1936
Art Duncan, D	1926–1927
Blake Dunlop, C	1983–1984

E

Bruce Eakin, C	1985–1986
Murray Eaves, C	1987–1988, 1989–1990
Tim Ecclestone, RW	1970–1971 to 1973–1974
Roy Edwards, G	1967–1968 to 1970–1971, 1972–1973 to 1973–1974
Pat Egan, D	1943–1944
Gerry Ehman, RW	1958–1959
Bo Elik, LW	1962–1963
Darren Eliot, G	1987–1988
Hap Emms, LW	1931–1932 to 1933–1934
Anders Eriksson, D	1995–1996 to 1998–1999
Bob Errey, LW	1995–1996 to 1996–1997
Bob Essensa, G	1993–1994
Chris Evans, D	1973–1974
Stu Evans, D	1930–1931, 1932–1933 to 1933–1934

F

Bob Falkenberg, D	1966–1967 to 1968–1969, 1970–1971 to 1971–1972
Alex Faulkner, C	1962–1963 to 1963–1964
Bernie Federko, C	1989–1990
Sergei Fedorov, C	1990–1991 to 2002–2003

Brent Fedyk, D	1987–1988 to 1991–1992
Lorne Ferguson, LW	1955–1956 to 1957–1958
Mark Ferner, D	1995
Viacheslav Fetisov, D	1995 to 1997–1998
Guyle Fielder, C	1952–1953, 1957–1958
Tom Filmore, RW	1930–1931 to 1931–1932
Jiri Fischer, D	1999–2000 to 2003–2004, 2005–2006
Dunc Fisher, RW	1958–1959
Joe Fisher, RW	1939–1940 to 1942–1943
Valtteri Flippula, F	2005–2006
Lee Fogolin, D	1947–1948 to 1950–1951
Rick Foley, D	1973–1974
Mike Foligno, RW	1979–1980 to 1981–1982
Bill Folk, D	1951–1952 to 1952–1953
Len Fontaine, RW	1972–1973 to 1973–1974
Val Fontaine, C-LW	1959–1960 to 1962–1963, 1964–1965 to 1966–1967
Dwight Foster, C	1982–1983 to 1985–1986
Yip Foster, D	1933–1934 to 1934–1935
Frank Foyston, C	1926–1927 to 1927–1928
Bobby Francis, C	1982–1983
Jimmy Franks, G	1936–1937 to 1937–1938, 1943–1944
Johan Franzen, F	2005–2006
Gord Fraser, D	1927–1928 to 1928–1929
Frank Frederickson, C	1926–1927, 1930–1931
Tim Friday, D	1985–1986
Miroslav Frycer, RW	1988–1989
Robbie Ftorek, C	1972–1973 to 1973–1974

G

Bill Gadsby, D	1961–1962 to 1965–1966
Jody Gage, RW	1980–1981 to 1981–1982, 1983–1984
Art Gagne, RW	1931–1932
Dave Gagner, G	1990–1991
Johnny Gallagher, D	1932–1933, 1936–1937
Gerard Gallant, LW	1984–1985 to 1992–1993

George Gardner, G	1965–1966 to 1967–1968
Danny Gare, RW	1981–1982 to 1985–1986
Johan Garpenlov, LW	1990–1991 to 1991–1992
Dave Gatherum, G	1953–1954
Fern Gauthier, RW	1945–1946 to 1948–1949
George Gee, C	1948–1949 to 1950–1951
Ed Giacomin, G	1975–1976 to 1977–1978
Gus Giesebrecht, C	1938–1939 to 1941–1942
Gilles Gilbert, G	1980–1981 to 1982–1983
Brent Gilchrist, C	1997–1998 to 2001–2002
Todd Gill, D	1998–1999,
	1999–2000 to 2000–2001
Art Giroux, RW	1935–1936
Larry Giroux, D	1974–1975 to 1977–1978
Lorry Gloeckner, D	1978–1979
Fred Glover, RW	1948–1949 to 1951–1952
Howie Glover, RW	1960–1961 to 1961–1962
Warren Godfrey, D	1955–1956 to 1961–1962,
	1963–1964 to 1967–1968
Pete Goegan, D	1957–1958 to 1966–1967
Bob Goldham, D	1950–1951 to 1955–1956
Leroy Goldsworthy, RW	1930–1931, 1932–1933
Yan Golubovsky, D	1997–1998 to 1999–2000
Ebbie Goodfellow, C-D	1929–1930 to 1942–1943
Fred Gordon, RW	1926–1927
Ted Graham, D	1933–1934 to 1934–1935
Danny Grant, LW	1974–1975 to 1977–1978
Doug Grant, G	1973–1974 to 1975–1976
Leo Gravelle, RW	1950–1951
Adam Graves, C	1987–1988 to 1989–1990
Gerry Gray, G	1970–1971
Harrison Gray, G	1963–1964
Red Green, LW	1928–1929
Rick Green, D	1990–1991
Stu Grimson, LW	1995 to 1996–1997
Lloyd Gross, LW	1933–1934 to 1934–1935
Don Grosso, C	1938–1939, 1944–1945
Danny Gruen, LW	1972–1973 to 1973–1974
Bep Guidolin, LW	1947–1948 to 1948–1949

H

Marc Habscheid, C-RW	1989–1990 to 1990–1991
Lloyd Haddon, D	1959–1960
Gord Haidy, RW	1949–1950
Slim Halderson, D	1926–1927
Len Haley, RW	1959–1960 to 1960–1961
Bob Halkidis, D	1993–1994 to 1995
Glenn Hall, G	1952–1953,
	1954–1955 to 1956–1957
Murray Hall, C	1964–1965 to 1966–1967
Doug Halward, D	1986–1987 to 1988–1989
Jean Hamel, D	1973–1974 to 1980–1981
Ted Hampson, C	1963–1964 to 1964–1965,
	1966–1967 to 1967–1968
Glen Hanlon, G	1986–1987 to 1990–1991
Dave Hanson, D	1978–1979
Emil Hanson, D	1932–1933
Terry Harper, D	1975–1976 to 1978–1979
Billy Harris, C	1965–1966
Ron Harris, D	1962–1963 to 1963–1964,
	1968–1969 to 1971–1972
Ted Harris, D	1973–1974
Gerry Hart, D	1968–1969 to 1971–1972
Harold Hart, LW	1926–1927
Buster Harvey, RW	1975–1976 to 1976–1977
Doug Harvey, D	1966–1967
Dominik Hasek, G	2001–2002, 2003–2004
Derian Hatcher, D	2003–2004
Ed Hatoum, RW	1968–1969 to 1969–1970
George Hay, C-LW	1927–1928 to 1930–1931,
	1932–1933
Jim Hay, D	1952–1953 to 1954–1955
Galen Head, RW	1967–1968
Rich Healey, D	1960–1961
Paul Henderson, LW	1962–1963 to 1967–1968
Jack Hendrickson, D	1957–1958 to 1958–1959,
	1961–1962
Jim Herberts, C	1928–1929 to 1929–1930
Art Herchenratter, C	1940–1941

Bryan Hextall, C	1975–1976	Earl Ingarfield, C-LW	1980–1981
Dennis Hextall, C	1975–1976 to 1978–1979	Ron Ingram, D	1963–1964
Glenn Hicks, LW	1979–1980 to 1980–1981		
Harold Hicks, D	1929–1930 to 1930–1931	**J**	
Tim Higgins, RW	1986–1987 to 1988–1989	Hal Jackson, D	1940–1941,
Dutch Hiller, LW	1941–1942		1942–1943 to 1946–1947
Jim Hiller, LW	1992–1993	Lou Jankowski, RW	1950–1951, 1952–1953
Larry Hillman, D	1954–1955 to 1956–1957	Gary Jarrett, LW	1966–1967 to 1967–1968
John Hilworth, D	1977–1978 to 1979–1980	Pierre Jarry, LW	1973–1974 to 1974–1975
Kevin Hodson, G	1995–1996 to 1998–1999	Larry Jeffrey, LW	1961–1962 to 1964–1965
Bill Hogaboam, C	1972–1973 to 1975–1976,	Bill Jennings, RW	1940–1941 to 1943–1944
	1978–1979 to 1979–1980	Al Jensen, G	1980–1981
Ken Holland, G	1983–1984	Al Johnson, RW	1960–1961 to 1962–1963
Flash Hollett, D	1943–1944 to 1945–1946	Brian Johnson, RW	1983–1984
Bucky Hollingworth, D	1955–1956 to 1957–1958	Danny Johnson, C	1971–1972
Chuck Holmes, RW	1958–1959, 1961–1962	Earl Johnson, C	1953–1954
Hap Holmes, G	1926–1927 to 1927–1928	Greg Johnson, C	1993–1994 to 1996–1997
Tomas Holmstrom, LW	1996–1997 to 2002–2003,	Larry Johnston, D	1971–1972 to 1973–1974
	2005–2006	Ed Johnstone, RW	1983–1984,
John Holota, C	1942–1943, 1945–1946		1985–1986 to 1986–1987
Pete Horeck, RW-LW	1946–1947 to 1948–1949	Greg Joly, D	1976–1977 to 1982–1983
Doug Houda, D	1985–1986,	Buck Jones, D	1938–1939 to 1939–1940,
	1987–1988 to 1990–1991,		1941–1942
	1998–1999	Curtis Joseph, G	2002–2003 to 2003–2004
Gordie Howe, RW	1946–1947 to 1970–1971	Ed Joyal, C	1962–1963 to 1964–1965
Mark Howe, D	1992–1993 to 1995		
Syd Howe, C-LW	1934–1935 to 1945–1946	**K**	
Steve Hrymnak, D	1952–1953	Red Kane, D	1943–1944
Willie Huber, D	1978–1979 to 1982–1983	Al Karlander, C-LW	1969–1970 to 1972–1973
Jiri Hudler, C	2003–2004, 2005–2006	Jack Keating, LW	1938–1939 to 1939–1940
Ron Hudson, RW	1937–1938, 1939–1940	Duke Keats, C	1926–1927 to 1927–1928
Brent Hughes, D	1973–1974	Dave Kelly, RW	1976–1977
Rusty Hughes, D	1929–1930	Pete Kelly, RW	1935–1936 to 1938–1939
Brett Hull, RW	2001–2002 to 2003–2004	Red Kelly, D	1947–1948 to 1959–1960
Dennis Hull, LW	1977–1978	Forbes Kennedy, C	1957–1958 to 1959–1960,
			1961–1962
I		Sheldon Kennedy, RW	1989–1990 to 1993–1994
Miroslav Ihnacak, LW	1988–1989	Alan Kerr, RW	1991–1992
Peter Ing, G	1993–1994	Brian Kilrea, LW	1957–1958

Hec Kilrea, LW	1931–1932,	Claude Laforge, LW	1958–1959,
	1935–1936 to 1939–1940		1960–1961 to 1961–1962,
Ken Kilrea, C-LW	1939–1940 to 1941–1942,		1963–1964 to 1964–1965
	1943–1944	Roger Lafreniere, D	1962–1963
Wally Kilrea, C	1934–1935 to 1937–1938	Serge Lajeunesse, D	1970–1971 to 1972–1973
Kris King, RW	1987–1988 to 1988–1989	Hec Lalande, C	1957–1958
Scott King, G	1990–1991 to 1991–1992	Joe Lamb, LW	1937–1938
Mark Kirton, C	1980–1981 to 1982–1983	Mark Lamb, C	1986–1987
Kelly Kisio, C	1982–1983 to 1985–1986	Lane Lambert, RW	1983–1984 to
Hobie Kitchen, D	1926–1927		1985–1986
Petr Klima, LW-RW	1985–1986 to 1989–1990,	Marc Lamothe, G	2003–2004
	1998–1999	Robert Lang, C	2003–2004, 2005–2006
Mike Knuble, RW	1996–1997 to 1997–1998	Al Langlois, D	1963–1964 to 1964–1965
Joe Kocur, RW	1984–1985 to 1990–1991,	Darryl Laplante, C	1997–1998 to 1999–2000
	1996–1997 to 1999–2000	Martin Lapointe, RW	1991–1992 to 2000–2001
Ladislav Kohn, RW	2001–2002	Rick Lapointe, D	1975–1976 to 1976–1977
Steve Konroyd, D	1992–1993 to 1993–1994	Igor Larionov, C	1995–1996 to 1999–2000,
Vladimir Konstantinov, D	1991–1992 to 1996–1997		2000–2001 to 2002–2003
Tomas Kopecky, C	2005–2006	Reed Larson, D	1976–1977 to 1985–1986
Jim Korn, D	1979–1980 to 1981–1982	Brian Lavender, LW	1972–1973 to 1973–1974
Mike Korney, RW	1973–1974 to 1975–1976	Dan Lawson, RW	1967–1968 to 1968–1969
Chris Kotsopoulos, D	1989–1990	Reggie Leach, RW	1982–1983
Vyacheslav Kozlov, C	1991–1992 to 2000–2001	Jim Leavins, D	1985–1986
Dale Krentz, LW	1986–1987 to 1988–1989	Brett Lebda, D	2005–2006
Niklas Kronwall, D	2003–2004, 2005–2006	Fernand LeBlanc, RW	1976–1977 to 1978–1979
Jim Krulicki, LW	1970–1971	J. P. LeBlanc, C	1975–1976 to 1978–1979
Uwe Krupp, D	1998–1999 to 2001–2002	Rene Leclerc, RW	1968–1969, 1970–1971
Gord Kruppke, D	1990–1991,	Manny Legace, G	1999–2000 to 2002–2003
	1992–1993 to 1993–1994	Claude Legris, G	1980–1981 to 1981–1982
Mike Krushelnyski, LW-C	1995	Real Lemieux, LW	1966–1967
Dave Kryskow, LW	1974–1975	Tony Leswick, RW	1951–1952 to 1954–1955,
Mark Kumpel, RW	1986–1987 to 1987–1988		1957–1958
Maxim Kuznetsov, D	2000–2001 to 2001–2002	Dave Lewis, D	1986–1987 to 1987–1988
		Herb Lewis, LW	1928–1929 to 1938–1939
L		Nick Libett, LW	1967–1968 to 1978–1979
Leo Labine, RW	1960–1961 to 1961–1962	Tony Licari, RW	1946–1947
Dan Labraaten, LW	1978–1979 to 1980–1981	Nicklas Lidstrom, D	1991–1992 to 2003–2004,
Randy Ladouceur, D	1982–1983 to 1986–1987		2005–2006
Mark Laforest, G	1985–1986 to 1986–1987	Andreas Lilja, D	2005–2006

Ted Lindsay, LW	1944–1945 to 1956–1957, 1964–1965
Carl Liscombe, LW	1937–1938 to 1945–1946
Ed Litzenberger, RW	1961–1962
Bill Lochead, RW	1974–1975 to 1978–1979
Mark Lofthouse, RW	1981–1982 to 1982–1983
Claude Loiselle, C	1981–1982 to 1985–1986
Barry Long, D	1979–1980
Clem Loughlin, D	1926–1927 to 1927–1928
Ron Low, G	1977–1978
Larry Lozinski, G	1980–1981
Dave Lucas, D	1962–1963
Don Luce, C	1970–1971
Harry Lumley, G	1943–1944 to 1949–1950
Len Lunde, C-RW	1958–1959 to 1961–1962
Tord Lundstrom, LW	1973–1974
Pat Lundy, C	1945–1946 to 1948–1949
Chris Luongo, D	1990–1991
George Lyle, LW	1979–1980 to 1981–1982
Jack Lynch, D	1973–1974 to 1974–1975
Vic Lynn, D	1943–1944

M

Lowell MacDonald, RW	1961–1962 to 1964–1965
Parker MacDonald, LW	1960–1961 to 1966–1967
Bruce MacGregor, RW	1960–1961 to 1970–1971
Calum MacKay, LW	1946–1947, 1948–1949
Howard Mackie, RW	1936–1937 to 1937–1938
Don MacLean, F	2005–2006
Paul MacLean, RW	1988–1989
Rick MacLeish, LW	1983–1984
Brian MacLellan, LW	1991–1992
John MacMillan, LW	1963–1964 to 1964–1965
Jamie Macoun, D	1997–1998 to 1998–1999
Frank Mahovlich, LW	1967–1968 to 1970–1971, 1979–1980 to 1980–1981
Pete Mahovlich, C	1965–1966 to 1968–1969
Dan Maloney, LW	1975–1976 to 1977–1978
Steve Maltais, LW	1993–1994

Kirk Maltby, LW	1995–1996 to 2003–2004, 2005–2006
Randy Manery, D	1970–1971 to 1971–1972
Ken Mann, RW	1975–1976
Bob Manno, LW-D	1983–1984 to 1984–1985
Norm Maracle, G	1997–1998 to 1998–1999
Lou Marcon, D	1958–1959 to 1959–1960, 1962–1963
Gus Marker, RW	1932–1933 to 1933–1934
Brad Marsh, D	1990–1991 to 1991–1992
Gary Marsh, LW	1967–1968
Bert Marshall, D	1965–1966 to 1967–1968
Clare Martin, D	1949–1950 to 1950–1951
Pit Martin, C	1961–1962, 1963–1964 to 1965–1966
Don Martineau, RW	1975–1976 to 1976–1977
Steve Martinson, D	1987–1988
Charlie Mason, RW	1938–1939
Roland Matte, D	1929–1930
Gary McAdam, RW	1980–1981
Jud McAtee, LW	1943–1944 to 1944–1945
Stan McCabe, LW	1929–1930 to 1930–1931
Doug McCaig, D	1941–1942, 1945–1946 to 1947–1948
Rick McCann, C	1967–1968 to 1971–1972, 1974–1975
Tom McCarthy, LW	1956–1957 to 1958–1959
Darren McCarty, LW	1993–1994 to 2003–2004
Kevin McClelland, RW	1989–1990 to 1990–1991
Bob McCord, D	1965–1966 to 1967–1968
Dale McCourt, C	1977–1978 to 1981–1982
Bill McCreary, LW	1957–1958
Brad McCrimmon, D	1990–1991 to 1992–1993
Brian McCutcheon, LW	1974–1975 to 1976–1977
Ab McDonald, LW	1965–1966 to 1966–1967, 1971–1972
Bucko McDonald, D	1934–1935 to 1938–1939
Byron McDonald, LW	1939–1940, 1944–1945
Al McDonough, RW	1977–1978

Bill McDougall, C	1990–1991
Pete McDuffe, G	1975–1976
Mike McEwen, D	1985–1986
Jim McFadden, G	1946–1947 to 1950–1951
Bob McGill, D	1991–1992
Tom McGratton, G	1947–1948
Bert McInenly, LW	1930–1931 to 1931–1932
Jack McIntyre, LW	1957–1958 to 1959–1960
Doug McKay, LW	1949–1950
Randy McKay, RW	1988–1989 to 1990–1991
Walt McKechnie, C	1974–1975 to 1976–1977, 1981–1982 to 1982–1983
Tony McKegney, RW	1989–1990
Don McKenney, LW	1965–1966
Bill McKenzie, G	1973–1974 to 1974–1975
John McKenzie, RW	1959–1960 to 1960–1961
Andrew McKim, C	1995
Rollie McLenahan, D	1945–1946
Al McLeod, D	1973–1974
Don McLeod, G	1970–1971
Mike McMahon, D	1969–1970
Max McNab, C	1947–1948 to 1950–1951
Billy McNeill, RW	1956–1957 to 1959–1960, 1962–1963 to 1963–1964
Stu McNeill, C	1957–1958 to 1959–1960
Basil McRae, LW	1985–1986 to 1986–1987
Chris McRae, LW	1989–1990
Pat McReavy, LW	1941–1942
Harry Meeking, LW	1926–1927
Tom Mellor, D	1973–1974 to 1974–1975
Gerry Melnyk, C	1955–1956, 1959–1960 to 1960–1961
Barry Melrose, D	1983–1984, 1985–1986
Howie Menard, C	1963–1964
Glenn Merkosky, LW	1985–1986, 1989–1990
Corrado Micalef, G	1981–1982 to 1985–1986
Nick Mickoski, LW	1957–1958 to 1958–1959
Hugh Millar, D	1946–1947
Greg Millen, G	1991–1992
Kevin Miller, RW	1990–1991 to 1991–1992, 2003–2004
Perry Miller, D	1977–1978 to 1980–1981
Tom Miller, C	1970–1971
Eddie Mio, G	1983–1984 to 1985–1986
Dmitri Mironov, D	1997–1998
John Miszuk, D	1963–1964
Bill Mitchell, D	1963–1964
John Mokosak, D	1988–1989 to 1989–1990
Ron Moffatt, LW	1932–1933 to 1934–1935
Garry Monahan, LW	1969–1970
Hank Montieth, LW	1968–1969 to 1970–1971
Alfie Moore, G	1939–1940
Don Morrison, C	1947–1948 to 1948–1949
Jim Morrison, D	1959–1960
Rod Morrison, RW	1947–1948
Dean Morton, D	1989–1990
Gus Mortson, D	1958–1959
Alex Motter, D	1937–1938 to 1942–1943
John Mowers, G	1940–1941 to 1942–1943, 1946–1947
Mark Mowers, C	2003–2004, 2005–2006
Wayne Muloin, D	1963–1964
Don Murdoch, RW	1981–1982
Brian Murphy, C	1974–1975
Joe Murphy, C-RW	1986–1987 to 1989–1990
Larry Murphy, D	1996–1997 to 2000–2001
Ron Murphy, LW	1964–1965 to 1965–1966
Ken Murray, D	1972–1973
Terry Murray, D	1976–1977
Anders Myrvold, D	2003–2004

N

Jim Nahrgang, D	1974–1975 to 1976–1977
Vaclav Nedomansky, C-RW	1977–1978 to 1981–1982
Rick Newell, D	1972–1973 to 1973–1974
John Newman, C	1930–1931
Eddie Nicholson, D	1947–1948
Jim Niekamp, D	1970–1971 to 1971–1972

Jim Nill, D	1987–1988 to 1989–1990
Reg Noble, D	1927–1928 to 1932–1933
Ted Nolan, LW	1981–1982, 1983–1984
Lee Norwood, D	1986–1987 to 1990–1991
Hank Nowak, LW	1974–1975

O

Adam Oates, C	1985–1986 to 1988–1989
Russ Oatman, LW	1926–1927
Mike O'Connell, D	1985–1986 to 1989–1990
Gerry Odrowski, D	1960–1961 to 1962–1963
John Ogrodnick, LW	1979–1980 to 1986–1987, 1992–1993
Fredrik Olausson, D	2001–2002
Murray Oliver, C	1957–1958, 1959–1960 to 1960–1961
Dennis Olson, LW	1957–1958
Jimmy Orlando, D	1936–1937 to 1937–1938, 1939–1940 to 1942–1943
Mark Osborne, LW	1981–1982 to 1982–1983
Chris Osgood, G	1993–1994 to 2000–2001

P

Pete Palangio, LW	1927–1928
Brad Park, D	1983–1984 to 1984–1985
Joe Paterson, LW	1980–1981 to 1983–1984
George Patterson, RW	1934–1935
Butch Paul, C	1964–1965
Marty Pavelich, LW	1947–1948 to 1956–1957
Jim Pavese, D	1987–1988 to 1988–1989
Mark Pederson, LW	1993–1994
Bert Peer, RW	1939–1940
Bob Perreault, G	1958–1959
Jim Peters Jr., C	1964–1965 to 1967–1968
Jim Peters Sr., RW	1949–1950 to 1950–1951, 1953–1954
Brent Peterson, C	1978–1979 to 1981–1982
Gord Pettinger, C	1933–1934 to 1937–1938
Robert Picard, D	1989–1990

Alex Pirus, RW	1979–1980
Rob Plumb, LW	1977–1978 to 1978–1979
Nellie Podolsky, LW	1948–1949
Bud Poile, RW	1948–1949
Don Poile, C-RW	1954–1955, 1957–1958
Dennis Polonich, RW	1974–1975 to 1980–1981, 1982–1983
Poul Popiel, D	1968–1969 to 1969–1970
Marc Potvin, LW	1990–1991 to 1991–1992
Dean Prentice, LW	1965–1966 to 1968–1969
Noel Price, D	1961–1962
Keith Primeau, C-LW	1990–1991 to 1995–1996
Bob Probert, LW-RW	1985–1986 to 1993–1994
Andre Pronovost, LW	1962–1963 to 1964–1965
Marcel Pronovost, D	1949–1950 to 1964–1965
Metro Prystai, RW-C	1950–1951 to 1957–1958
Cliff Purpur, RW	1944–1945
Chris Pusey, G	1985–1986
Jamie Pushor, D	1995–1996 to 1997–1998
Nelson Pyatt, C	1973–1974 to 1974–1975

Q

Bill Quackenbush, D	1942–1943 to 1948–1949
Kyle Quincey, D	2005–2006

R

Yves Racine, D	1989–1990 to 1992–1993
Clare Raglan, D	1950–1951
Mike Ramsey, D	1995–1996, 1996–1997
Bill Ranford, G	1998–1999
Matt Ravlich, D	1969–1970
Marc Reaume, D	1959–1960 to 1960–1961
Billy Reay, C	1943–1944 to 1944–1945
Mickey Redmond, RW	1970–1971 to 1975–1976
Dutch Reibel, C	1953–1954 to 1957–1958
Gerry Reid, C	1948–1949
Leo Reise, D	1946–1947 to 1951–1952
Dave Richardson, LW	1967–1968
Terry Richardson, G	1973–1974 to 1976–1977

Steve Richmond, D	1985–1986
Vincent Riendeau, G	1991–1992 to 1993–1994
Dennis Riggin, G	1959–1960, 1962–1963
Jim Riley, RW	1926–1927
Bob Ritchie, LW	1976–1977 to 1977–1978
Jamie Rivers, D	2003–2004
Wayne Rivers, RW	1961–1962
John Ross Roach, G	1932–1933 to 1934–1935
Phil Roberto, RW	1974–1975 to 1975–1976
Doug Roberts, RW	1965–1966 to 1967–1968, 1973–1974 to 1974–1975
Earl Robertson, G	1936–1937
Fred Robertson, D	1933–1934
Torrie Robertson, LW	1988–1989 to 1989–1990
Nathan Robinson, C	2003–2004
Luc Robitaille, LW	2001–2002 to 2002–2003
Mike Robitaille, D	1970–1971
Desse Roche, RW	1934–1935
Earle Roche, LW	1934–1935
Dave Rochefort, C	1966–1967
Leon Rochefort, RW	1971–1972 to 1972–1973
Harvey Rockburn, D	1929–1930 to 1930–1931
Marc Rodgers, RW	1999–2000
Stacy Roest, C	1998–1999 to 1999–2000
Dale Rolfe, D	1969–1970 to 1970–1971
Rollie Rossignol, LW	1943–1944, 1945–1946
Rolly Roulston, D	1936–1937
Bob Rouse, D	1995 to 1997–1998
Tom Rowe, RW	1982–1983
Bernie Ruelle, LW	1943–1944
Pat Rupp, G	1963–1964
Jimmy Rutherford, G	1970–1971, 1973–1974 to 1980–1981, 1982–1983

S

Andre St. Laurent, C	1977–1978 to 1978–1979, 1983–1984
Sam St. Laurent, G	1986–1987 to 1989–1990

Borje Salming, D	1989–1990
Barry Salovaara, D	1974–1975 to 1975–1976
Mikael Samuelsson, F	2005–2006
Ulf Samuelsson, D	1998–1999
Tomas Sandstrom, RW-LW	1996–1997
Ed Sanford, C	1955–1956
Bob Sauve, G	1981–1982
Terry Sawchuk, G	1949–1950 to 1954–1955, 1957–1958 to 1963–1964, 1968–1969
Kevin Schamehorn, RW	1976–1977, 1979–1980
Mathieu Schneider, D	2002–2003 to 2003–2004, 2005–2006
Jim Schoenfeld, D	1981–1982 to 1982–1983
Dwight Schofield, D	1976–1977
Enio Sclisizzi, LW	1946–1947 to 1949–1950, 1951–1952
Earl Seibert, D	1944–1945 to 1945–1946
Ric Seiling, RW	1986–1987
Brendan Shanahan, LW	1996–1997 to 2003–2004, 2005–2006
Daniel Shank, RW	1989–1990 to 1990–1991
Jeff Sharples, D	1986–1987 to 1988–1989
Doug Shedden, RW	1985–1986 to 1986–1987
Bobby Sheehan, C	1976–1977
Tim Sheehy, RW	1977–1978
Frank Sheppard, C	1927–1928
John Sheppard, LW	1926–1927 to 1927–1928
Ray Sheppard, RW	1991–1992 to 1995
John Sherf, LW	1935–1936 to 1938–1939, 1943–1944
Gord Sherritt, D	1943–1944
Jim Shires, LW	1970–1971
Steve Short, D	1978–1979
Gary Shuchuk, RW	1990–1991
Dave Silk, RW	1984–1985
Mike Sillinger, C	1990–1991 to 1995
Cully Simon, D	1942–1943 to 1944–1945
Thain Simon, D	1946–1947

Cliff Simpson, C	1946–1947 to 1947–1948
Reg Sinclair, RW	1952–1953
Darryl Sittler, C-LW	1984–1985
Bjorne Skaare, C	1978–1979
Glen Skov, C	1949–1950 to 1954–1955
Jiri Slegr, D	2001–2002
Al Smith, G	1971–1972
Alex Smith, D	1931–1932
Brad Smith, RW	1980–1981 to 1984–1985
Brian Smith, LW	1957–1958, 1960–1961
Carl Smith, LW	1943–1944
Derek Smith, C	1981–1982 to 1982–1983
Floyd Smith, RW	1962–1963 to 1967–1968
Greg Smith, D	1981–1982 to 1985–1986
Nakina Dalton Smith, LW	1943–1944
Normie Smith, G	1934–1935, 1938–1939,
	1943–1944 to 1944–1945
Rick Smith, D	1980–1981
Ted Snell, RW	1974–1975
Harold Snepsts, D	1985–1986 to 1987–1988
Sandy Snow, RW	1968–1969
Dennis Sobchuk, C	1979–1980
Ken Solheim, LW	1982–1983
Bob Solinger, LW	1959–1960
John Sorrell, LW	1930–1931 to 1937–1938
Fred Speck, C	1968–1969 to 1969–1970
Ted Speers, RW	1985–1986
Irv Spencer, D-LW	1963–1964 to 1965–1966,
	1967–1968
Ron Stackhouse, D	1971–1972 to 1973–1974
Ed Stankiewicz, LW	1953–1954, 1955–1956
Wilf Starr, C	1933–1934 to 1935–1936
Vic Stasiuk, RW-LW	1950–1951 to 1954–1955,
	1960–1961 to 1962–1963
Ray Staszak, RW	1985–1986
Frank Steele, LW	1930–1931
Greg Stefan, G	1981–1982 to 1989–1990
Pete Stemkowski, C	1967–1968 to 1970–1971

"Black" Jack Stewart, D	1938–1939 to 1942–1943,
	1945–1946 to 1949–1950
Blair Stewart, LW	1973–1974 to 1974–1975
Gaye Stewart, LW	1950–1951
Gord Strate, D	1956–1957 to 1958–1959
Art Stratton, C	1963–1964
Herb Stuart, G	1926–1927
Barry Sullivan, RW	1947–1948
Bill Sutherland, LW	1971–1972

T

John Taft, D	1978–1979
Jean-Guy Talbot, D	1967–1968
Chris Tancil, C	1991–1992 to 1992–1993
Billy Taylor, C	1946–1947
Ted Taylor, LW	1966–1967
Tim Taylor, LW	1993–1994 to 1996–1997
Harvey Teno, G	1938–1939
Larry Thibeault, LW	1944–1945
Steve Thomas, RW	2003–2004
Cecil Thompson, G	1938–1939 to 1939–1940
Errol Thompson, LW	1977–1978 to 1980–1981
Billy Thomson, RW	1938–1939, 1943–1944
Jerry Toppazzini, RW	1955–1956
Larry Trader, D	1982–1983, 1984–1985
Percy Traub, D	1927–1928 to 1928–1929
Dave Trottier, LW	1938–1939
Joe Turner, G	1941–1942

U

Norm Ullman, C	1955–1956 to 1967–1968
Garry Unger, C	1967–1968 to 1970–1971

V

Rogie Vachon, G	1978–1979 to 1979–1980
Eric Vail, LW	1981–1982
Rick Vasko, D	1979–1980 to 1980–1981
Darren Veitch, D	1985–1986 to 1987–1988

Pat Verbeek, RW	1999–2000 to 2000–2001
Mike Vernon, G	1995 to 1996–1997
Dennis Vial, D	1990–1991 to 1992–1993
Doug Volmer, RW	1969–1970 to 1971–1972
Carl Voss, C	1932–1933

W

Jack Walker, LW	1926–1927 to 1927–1928
Bob Wall, D	1964–1965 to 1966–1967, 1971–1972
Jesse Wallin, D	1999–2000, 2000–2001 to 2002–2003
Wes Walz, C	1995–1996
Aaron Ward, D	1993–1994 to 2000–2001
Eddie Wares, RW	1937–1938 to 1942–1943
Bryan Watson, D	1965–1966 to 1966–1967, 1973–1974 to 1976–1977
Harry Watson, LW	1942–1943, 1945–1946
Jim Watson, D	1963–1964 to 1965–1966, 1967–1968 to 1969–1970
Brian Watts, LW	1975–1976
Tom Webster, RW	1970–1971 to 1971–1972, 1979–1980
Cooney Weiland, C	1933–1934 to 1934–1935
Stan Weir, C	1982–1983
Carl Wetzel, G	1964–1965
Bob Whitelaw, D	1940–1941 to 1941–1942
Ray Whitney, LW	2003–2004
Archie Wilder, LW	1940–1941
Bob Wilkie, D	1990–1991
Burr Williams, D	1933–1934, 1936–1937
Carl Williams, D	1931–1932
Dave "Tiger" Williams, LW	1984–1985
Fred Williams, C	1976–1977
Jason Williams, C	2000–2001 to 2003–2004, 2005–2006

Johnny Wilson, LW	1949–1950 to 1954–1955, 1957–1958 to 1958–1959
Larry Wilson, C	1949–1950, 1951–1952 to 1952–1953
Rick Wilson, D	1976–1977
Ross "Lefty" Wilson, G	1953–1954
Murray Wing, D	1973–1974
Eddie Wiseman, RW	1932–1933 to 1935–1936
Steve Wochy, C-RW	1944–1945, 1946–1947
Benny Woit, D	1950–1951 to 1954–1955
Mike Wong, C	1975–1976
Paul Woods, LW	1977–1978 to 1983–1984
Jason Woolley, D	2002–2003 to 2003–2004, 2005–2006
Ken Wregget, G	1999–2000
Larry Wright, RW-C	1977–1978

Y

Jason York, D	1992–1993 to 1995
B. J. Young, RW	1999–2000
Doug Young, D	1931–1932 to 1938–1939
Howie Young, D	1960–1961 to 1962–1963, 1966–1967 to 1967–1968
Warren Young, LW	1985–1986
Paul Ysebaert, LW	1990–1991 to 1992–1993
Steve Yzerman, C	1983–1984 to 2003–2004, 2005–2006

Z

Larry Zeidel, D	1951–1952 to 1952–1953
Ed Zeniuk, D	1954–1955
Henrik Zetterberg, C	2002–2003 to 2003–2004, 2005–2006
Rick Zombo, D	1984–1985 to 1991–1992
Rudy Zunich, D	1943–1944

About the Author

Nicholas J. Cotsonika covered the Red Wings for the *Detroit Free Press* from 1999 to 2004. Born and raised in the Detroit area, he attended the University of Michigan. He co-edited "We're No. 1," a *Michigan Daily* chronicle of the Wolverines' 1997 national football championship, served as the main author of *Century of Champions*, a Free Press book celebrating 100 years of Michigan sports memories, and wrote *Hockey Gods*, an inside look at the Wings' 2002 Stanley Cup season. His work has appeared in four other Free Press books and several other publications, including *The Hockey News*, *The Washington Post* and *Sports Illustrated*. He lives with his wife, Alison, and their son, Jacob, in Ann Arbor, Michigan.